bush theatre
vale PRODUCTIONS

Strawberry Vale Productions
in association with the Bush Theatre
presents the world premiere of

Eigengrau

by Penelope Skinner

10 March – 10 April 2010

Cast

Tim Muffin	John Cummins
Rose	Sinead Matthews
Cassie	Alison O'Donnell
Mark	Geoffrey Streatfeild

Creative Team

Writer	Penelope Skinner
Director	Polly Findlay
Designer	Hannah Clark
Lighting Designer	Matthew Pitman
Sound Designer	Rich Walsh
Costume Supervisor	Liz Evans
Producer	Lilli Geissendorfer
Stage Manager	Bonnie Morris
Assistant Director	Tim Hoare
Assistant Stage Manager	Adam McElderry
Design Assistant	Alison Neighbour
	Christopher Rosewell

The Bush Theatre would like to give particular thanks
to aka, West 12 Shopping Centre and Westfield London;
and Strawberry Vale would like to thank Heinz Ackermann, Lorna Beckett,
Leo Bill, All staff at the Bush Theatre, Faye Castelowe, Peter Clayton,
Mark Grimmer, Titas Halder, Harry Hadden-Paton, Sam Hodges, Ed Hogg,
Juliet Horsley, Sophie Hunter, Joyce Hytner, Sarah Ingram, Angus Jackson,
Hywel John, Eddie Keogh, Leila and Nadia Latif, Henri Lambert, John Leonard,
Eleanor Lloyd, Hugh Lloyd-Jukes, Lyndsey Marshal, Barbara Matthews,
Luke McEwan, Michael Mears, Harry Melling, James Midgley, Purni Morell,
Sarah Nicholson, Clare Parsons, Matthew Poxon, Susan Radhakrishnan,
George Rainsford, Richard Scarborough, Vaughan Sivell, Clare Slater,
Giles Smart, Wendy Spon, Emma Stenning, Theatre503, Jack Thorne,
Charlie Tims, Pam Wilson, Western Edge Plays, Diccon Wright and 59 Productions.

Strawberry Vale and the Bush would like to thank Hew at the National Theatre

Company

John Cummins (Tim)

Theatre includes: *The Good Soul of Szechuan* (Manchester Library Theatre), *A Stab In The Dark* (Kings Head/Latitude Festival), *Our Country's Good* (The Watermill), *Edward II* (B.A.C.), *Pains of Youth* (Belgrade), *Romeo and Juliet* (B.A.C.), *The Reporter*, *The Alchemist* (National Theatre), *The Strindberg Project* (National Theatre Studio), *The Beaver Coat* (The Finborough).

Television includes: *Eastenders*, *Holby City*, *Doctors*, *Banged up Abroad*.

Radio includes: *London Calling*, *To Sicken And So Die*, *A Fare To Remember*, *Small Gods*, *Twice Brightly*, *Hold My Breath*, *The Voice of God*, *Troilus and Cressida*, *The Fountain Overflows*, *Agatha Rasin*, *Clare in the Community*.

Sinead Matthews (Rose)

Theatre includes: *Our Class* (National Theatre), *His Ghostly Heart*, *Little Dolls* (Bush Theatre)), *Women Of Troy* (National Theatre), *The Wild Duck* (Donmar),*You Never Can Tell* (Bath & Tour/West End), *The Birthday Party* (West End), *The Mandate* (Royal National), *The Crucible* (Crucible), *Spoonface Steinberg* (GBS).

Film includes: *Wreckers*, *Nanny McPhee 2*, *The Boat That Rocked*, *Spring Of 1941*, *Happy Go Lucky*, *Wednesday* (short), *Pride and Prejudice*, *Vera Drake*.

Television includes: *Men Are Wonderful*, *Half Broken Things*, *Ideal x 6*, *Trial and Retribution*, *Who Gets The Dog*, *The Hogfather*, *Viva Las Blackpool*, *He Knew He Was Right*.

Alison O'Donnell (Cassie)

Theatre includes: *Dolls* (National Theatre of Scotland/Hush Productions), *The Assassination Of Paris Hilton* (Racked), *Lady Windermere's Fan* (A Play, A Pie and A Pint), *And The Act Going Home Tonight Is*, *Skin*, *Henry's Hangover*, *Scrabble*, *Reunion* (DryWrite), *Mad Funny Just* (Creased), *1 In 5* (Hampstead Theatre Daring Pairings), *Phaedre* (Offstage), *Barren* (Old Vic New Voices – The 24 Hour Plays), *The Ghost Sonata* (Goat and Monkey), *Broken Road* (Hush Productions), *Love Sex & Cider* (Jacuzzi Theatre).

Geoffrey Streatfeild (Mark)

Theatre includes: *The Contingency Plan: On the Beach and Resilience* (Bush Theatre); *Pains of Youth, The History Boys, The Bacchai* (National); *Journey's End* (West End); *Henry VI Parts 1, 2 & 3, Richard III, Henry IV Parts 1 & 2, Henry V* (RSC); *Nathan the Wise, Merchant of Venice* (Chichester).

TV includes: *Ashes to Ashes, Hunter, Elizabeth I, 20,000 Streets Under the Sky, Midsomer Murders, Timewatch, The Other Boleyn Girl, Love in a Cold Climate, Sword of Honour.*

Film includes: *Angel, Matchpoint, Kinky Boots.*

Hannah Clark (Designer)

Hannah trained in theatre design at Nottingham Trent University and Central School of Speech and Drama. She was a winner of the 2005 Linbury Biennial Prize for stage design.

Designs include: *2nd May 1997* (Bush Theatre), *A Midsummer Night's Dream* (The Globe); *Knives In Hens, Thyestes, Torn* (Arcola), *Under Milk Wood* (Northampton Theatre Royal), *Nocturnal, Big Love* (The Gate), *Billy Wonderful* (Liverpool Everyman), *Company , Hortensia And The Museum Of Dreams* (RADA), *The Snow Queen* (West Yorkshire Playhouse), *Proper Clever* (Liverpool Playhouse), *Pequenas Delicias* (Requardt & Company), *Roadkill Cafe* (Requardt & Company, Centro Coreográfico de Montemor-o-Novo, Portugal / Teatro Fondamenta Nuove, Venice / The Place), *House Of Agnes* (Paines Plough), *Breakfast With Mugabe* (Theatre Royal Bath), *The Cracks In My Skin, Who's Afraid Of Virginia Woolf?* (Manchester Royal Exchange), *Othello* (Salisbury Playhouse), *As You Like It, We That Are Left* (Watford Palace Theatre), *Terre Haute* (Assembly Rooms, Edinburgh / Trafalgar Studios / UK Tour / 59E59, New York), *The Taming Of The Shrew* (Bristol Old Vic), *Jammy Dodgers* (Requardt & Company, The Place / Royal Opera House 2 / INT Tour).

Polly Findlay (Director)

Polly trained at LAMDA and at the National Theatre Studio. She was the winner of the 2007 JMK Award for Young Directors, and was the recipient of the 2006/7 Bulldog Princeps Bursary at the National Theatre Studio. Directing credits include *Thyestes* (Arcola Theatre), *Romeo and Juliet* (BAC), MIC:roscope (Lilian Baylis, Sadler's Wells), *Good* (Sound Theatre), *As You Like It* (Oxford Playhouse). Assisting credits include *Warhorse* (Olivier, National Theatre), *The Man of Mode* (Olivier, National Theatre), *The Seafarer* (Cottesloe, National Theatre).

Tim Hoare (Assistant Director)

Theatre as Director includes: *BASH* (Curtains Up Barons Court); *Henry V* (Trafalgar Studios and Rustavelli National Theatre Tbilisi); *A Few Good Men* (Oxford Playhouse).

Theatre as Assistant Director includes: *Slaves* (Theatre503).

Tim has a BA (Hons) in English from Oxford University, and has recently been selected for the director traineeship at the Chichester Festival Theatre.

Matthew Pitman (Lighting Designer)

Lighting Designer: *Company* (Rada), *Thyestes* (Arcola Theatre), *Edward II* (BAC), *Paradise Lost* (Southwalk Playhouse), *Romeo and Juliet* (BAC), *More Light* (National Theatre – Olivier), *Connections* Festivals 2006/7 (National Theatre)

Associate: *Seafarer* (National Theatre & Tour), *Measure4Measure* (Complicite Tour), *The UN Inspector* (National Theatre), *Royal Hunt of the Sun* (National Theatre).

Upcoming projects include: *Light Shining in Buckinghamshire* (Arcola), *The Half Light* (film).

Penelope Skinner (Writer)

Writing credits include: *Fucked* (Old Red Lion/Assembly Rooms Edinburgh); *Scarlet's Circus* (Hampstead Theatre Heat & Light Company); *The Old Road: A Man in Black Mystery* (BBC Radio 7); *1 in 5* (Hampstead Theatre - Upstart); *Scratch* (Locative drama for Radio 3 Free Thinking Festival); *The Art Room* (a comic).

Rich Walsh (Sound Designer)

Previous sound designs include: *The Observer, Baby Girl, DNA, The Miracle, The Five Wives Of Maurice Pinder, Landscape With Weapon, The Reporter, The Alchemist, Exiles, Southwark Fair, The Mandate, Primo, The False Servant, Sing Yer Heart Out For The Lads, Scenes From The Big Picture, Dinner, Closing Time, The Associate, Sanctuary, The Mentalists, The Shadow Of A Boy, Free, The Walls* (National Theatre); *Exposure, Under The Blue Sky, On Raftery's Hill, Sacred Heart, Trust, Choice* (Royal Court); *Primo* (Music Box Theatre – Broadway & Hampstead Theatre); *Dinner* (Wyndhams); *What The Night Is For* (Comedy); *50 Revolutions* (Whitehall); *Rock, Fimbles Live!, The Unexpected Man, The Lady In The Van, The Deep Blue Sea, The Boy Who Left Home, The Nation's Favourite – The True Adventures Of Radio One* (UK Tours); *The Price, Hyperlynx* (Tricycle Theatre); *Julie Burchill Is Away...* (Soho Theatre); *Kingfisher Blue* (Bush Theatre); *Cue Deadly, Yllana's 666* (Riverside Studios); *Strike Gently Away From Body* (Young Vic Studio); *The Difficult Unicorn* (Southwark Playhouse); *Small Craft Warnings* (The Pleasance – London); *Dirk* (The Oxford Playhouse). Rich was Associate Sound Designer for *The Cat In The Hat* (National Theatre).

Strawberry Vale Productions

Strawberry Vale is an independent film and theatre production company based in London, UK and Cologne, Germany run by sisters Hana and Lilli Geissendorfer. Since 2006, Strawberry Vale has produced three short films and five plays, and been part of numerous creative collaborations.

Theatre production and co-production credits include the disquieting interrogation of the Bulger case, *Monsters* by Niklas Radstrom (dir. Christopher Haydon, with Arcola at Arcola 2009), the hydrogen fuel-cell powered, ecologically sustainable *The Living Unknown Soldier* (dir. Sebastian Armesto, with simple8 at Arcola 2008), the delicate female monologue *Limbo* by Declan Feenan (dir. Dan Sherer, with Real Circumstance at Underbelly Edinburgh, York Theatre Royal, Arcola, 2007), Owen McCafferty's boisterous *Mojo Mickybo* (dir. Jonathan Humphreys at Trafalgar Studios 2007) and Buzz Goodbody's adaptation of *Notes from Underground* by Fyodor Dostoyevsky (dir. Christopher Haydon at Arcola, 2006-7).

Strawberry Vale seeks to develop and deliver innovative, socially conscious theatre, and is committed to its three Creative Associates, directors Polly Findlay, Fiona Morrell and Christopher Haydon.

Film credits include *Playtime* (2007, 10mins/35mm Winner, Best Short Film for a Teenage Audience, 24th International Interfilm Short Film Festival in Berlin), *Marion* (2008, 23mins/35mm) and *Hermann* (2010, forthcoming), all written and directed by Hana Geissendorfer.

To find out more about our work,
and how you can get involved and support us,
please visit

www.strawberryvaleproductions.com

The Bush Theatre

'One of the most experienced prospectors of raw talent in Europe'
The Independent

Since its inception in 1972, the Bush Theatre has pursued its singular vision of discovery, risk and entertainment from its home in Shepherds Bush. That vision is valued and embraced by a community of audience and artists radiating out from our distinctive corner of West London across the world. The Bush is a local theatre with an international reputation. Since its beginning, the Bush has produced hundreds of groundbreaking premieres, many of them Bush commissions, and hosted guest productions by leading companies and artists from across the world. On any given night, those queuing at the foot of our stairs to take their seats could have travelled from Auckland or popped in from round the corner.

What draws them to the Bush is the promise of a good night out and our proven commitment to launch, from our stage, successive generations of playwrights and artists. Samuel Adamson, David Eldridge, Jonathan Harvey, Catherine Johnson, Tony Kushner, Stephen Poliakoff, Jack Thorne and Victoria Wood (all then unknown) began their careers at the Bush. The unwritten contract between talent and risk is understood by actors who work at the Bush, creating roles in untested new plays. Unique amongst local theatres, the Bush consistently draws actors of the highest reputation and calibre. Joseph Fiennes and Ian Hart recently took leading roles in a first play by an unknown playwright to great critical success. John Simm and Richard Wilson acted in premieres both of which transferred into the West End. The Bush has won over 100 awards, and developed an enviable reputation for touring its acclaimed productions nationally and internationally.

Audiences and organisations far beyond our stage profit from the risks we take. The value attached to the Bush by other theatres and by the film and television industries is both significant and considerable. The Bush receives more than 1,000 scripts through the post every year, and reads and responds to them all. This is one small part of a comprehensive playwrights' development programme which nurtures the relationship between writer and director, as well as playwright residencies and commissions. Everything that we do to develop playwrights focuses them towards a production on our stage or beyond.

We have also launched an ambitious new education, training and professional development programme, bushfutures, providing opportunities for different sectors of the community and professionals to access the expertise of Bush playwrights, directors, designers, technicians and actors, and to play an active role in influencing the future development of the theatre and its programme. Last year saw the launch of our new social networking and online publishing website **www.bushgreen.org**. The site is a great new forum for playwrights and theatre people to meet, share experiences and collaborate. Through this pioneering work, the Bush will reach and connect with new writers and new audiences.

Josie Rourke, Artistic Director

At the Bush Theatre

Artistic Director	**Josie Rourke**
Executive Director	**Angela Bond**
Associate Directors	**Nathan Curry**
	Charlotte Gwinner
Associate Director – bushfutures	**Anthea Williams**
Production Manager	**Anthony Newton**
Acting Marketing Manager	**Sophie Coke-Steel**
Producers	**Caroline Dyott**
	Tara Wilkinson
Development Officers	**Bethany Ann McDonald**
	Leonora Twynam
Company Stage Manager	**Angela Riddell**
Bookkeeper	**Ella Rule**
Box Office and Front of House Manager	**Clare Moss**
Box Office Assistants	**Kirsty Cox, Alex Hern,**
	Ava Leman Morgan,
	Kate McGregor, Amanda Ramasawmy,
	Lee Simpson
Press Representative	**Ewan Thomson**
Intern	**Kirsty Patrick Ward**
Assistant to the Directors	**Liz Eddy**
Composer in Residence	**Michael Bruce**
Front of House Duty Managers	**Kirsty Cox, Alex Hern, Laurelle Jones,**
	Ava Leman Morgan, Lucy McCann,
	Jen Vile, Kirsty Patrick Ward
Duty Technicians	**Vivienne Clavering, Ben Sherratt**
Associate Artists	**Tanya Burns, Arthur Darvill,**
	Chloe Emmerson, James Farncombe,
	Richard Jordan, Emma Laxton,
	Paul Miller, Lucy Osborne
Creative Associates	**Clare Lizzimore, George Perrin,**
	Hamish Pirie, Titas Halder
Associate Playwright	**Anthony Weigh**
Pearson Playwright	**Nick Payne**

The Bush Theatre has the support of the Pearson Playwrights' Scheme
sponsored by the Peggy Ramsay Foundation

The Bush Theatre, Shepherds Bush Green, London W12 8QD
Box Office: 020 8743 5050   www.bushtheatre.co.uk

The Alternative Theatre Company Ltd. (The Bush Theatre)
is a Registered Charity no. 270080

Company registration no. 1221968   VAT no. 228 3168 73

Supported by
ARTS COUNCIL ENGLAND

supported by
h&f
hammersmith & fulham

Be There at the Beginning

The Bush Theatre would like to say a very special 'Thank You' to the following supporters, corporate sponsors and trusts and foundations, whose valuable contributions continue to help us nurture, develop and present some of the brightest new literary stars and theatre artists.

If you are interested in finding out how to be involved, visit the 'Support Us' section of our website, email development@bushtheatre.co.uk or call 020 8743 3584.

Lone Star
Eric Abraham and
Sigrid Rausing
Gianni Alen-Buckley
Catherine Johnson

Handful of Stars
Anonymous
Jim Broadbent
Clyde Cooper
David and Alexander
Emmerson
Tom Erhardt
Julia Foster
Richard and Elizabeth
Phillips
Alan Rickman
John and Tita Shakeshaft

Glee Club
Anonymous
John Botrill
David Brooks
Maggie Burrows
Clive Butler
Mike Figgis
Vivien Goodwin
Virginia Ironside
Adam Kenwright
Neil LaBute
Antonia Lloyd
Michael McCoy
Judith Mellor
John and Jacqui Pearson
Mr and Mrs Alan Radcliffe
Radfin Courier Service
John Reynolds
Susie Sainsbury
Brian D Smith
Abigail Uden

Corporate Sponsors
The Agency (London) Ltd
Harbottle & Lewis LLP
Ludgate Environmental Ltd
Curtis Brown Group Ltd
West12 Shopping &
Leisure Centre
Westfield London
Markson Pianos

Trusts and Foundations
The Daisy Trust
The D'Oyly Carte
Charitable Trust
The Earls Court &
Olympia Charitable Trust
The Elizabeth & Gordon
Bloor Charitable
Foundation
The Eranda Foundation
Garfield Weston
Foundation
The Gatsby Charitable
Foundation
Haberdashers'
Benevolent Foundation
The Harold Hyam Wingate
Foundation
Jerwood Charitable
Foundation
The John Thaw
Foundation
The Laurie & Gillian
Marsh Charitable Trust
The Marina Kleinwort
Trust
The Martin Bowley
Charitable Trust
Old Possum's Practical
Trust
The Peggy Ramsay
Foundation
The Thistle Trust
The Peter Wolff Theatre
Trust
Split Infinitive Trust
The 2011 Trust

The Bush Theatre has recently launched **bushgreen**, a social networking website for people in theatre to connect, collaborate and publish plays in innovative ways. The mission of **bushgreen** is to connect playwrights with theatre practitioners, plays with producers to promote best practice and inspire the creation of exciting new theatre.

bushgreen allows members to:

- Submit plays directly to the Bush for our team to read and consider for production

- Connect with other writers, directors, producers and theatres

- Publish scripts online so more people can access your work

- Purchse scripts from hundreds of new playwrights

There are thousands of members and hundreds of plays on the site.

To join log on to **www.bushgreen.org**

Penelope Skinner

Eigengrau

faber and faber

First published in 2010
by Faber and Faber Limited
74–77 Great Russell Street, London WC1B 3DA

Typeset by Country Setting, Kingsdown, Kent CT14 8ES
Printed and bound by CPI Group (UK) Ltd, Croydon, CR0 4YY

A CIP record for this book
is available from the British Library

ISBN 978–0–571–25596–2

2 4 6 8 10 9 7 5 3

Acknowledgements

Giles Smart, Polly Findlay, Lilli Geissendorfer and the cast. Josie Rourke, Tara Wilkinson and all the staff at the Bush Theatre. Tim Hoare and Bonnie Morris. Purni Morell, Clare Slater and everyone at the National Theatre Studio. All the actors who've taken part in readings, especially the first ever read-through: Claire Murphy, Becci Gemmell, Janey Lawson, Joseph Arkley and Richard Pepper. For advice and support: Janfarie, Andrew, Ginny, Andy, and other assorted Skinners etc. Natalie Donbavand, AOD, Victoria Ward, Faith Miles, Kate Penning, Emma Stonex, Jack Thorne and Steve King. Thanks to Kat Banyard, Anna van Heeswijk, Sandrine Leveque, Emma Crowe, JOD and all feminists, young and old. And finally thank you Betty. For how you loved me.

Characters

Tim Muffin
a fat bloke

Cassie
a feminist activist

Rose
a believer

Mark
the marketing guy

EIGENGRAU

For Ben

Punctuation

/
indicates an interrupted line

. . .
indicates the word / line should be protracted

(   )
indicates words which are not heard or not spoken

No punctuation at the end of a line
indicates that the thought is not finished

The layout and position of new lines give
some indication of thought processes and rhythm.
A new line may mean a new thought, or it may
mean the word on the new line took some time
to think of

I

EASTBOURNE PIER

Tim stands on the end of Eastbourne Pier. Seagulls caw.
Somewhere in the background, the jangle of the arcade
machines. And below, the wash of the sea on the stony
beach.
  It is cold.
  Tim holds a large porcelain cat, with a removable
head. He unscrews the lid and goes to remove it.

Tim I came into the living room and you were sitting on
the sofa having a fag and you'd made a cake and the tea
was in the pot and I walked over to you and I looked at
you and I said I knew it. I knew you weren't really dead.
I knew you wouldn't leave me.

  And then I woke up.

  He looks at the urn.
  He shivers.

Bit cold though. Isn't it?

  He tightens the head back up again.
  Blackout.

2

CASSIE AND ROSE'S FLAT

Cassie is working on her laptop in the living room. Mark
enters, not wearing his shirt.
  His shirt is, in fact, on Cassie's chair.

Mark Shit. Sorry / I thought I was the only one here.

Cas Hi.
　No.

Mark Rose said you'd be at work.

Cas I sort of
　am.

Mark Oh right. Sorry.

Cas It's OK. Sorry are you
　Mark?

Mark Yes. Fuck. Mark. You / must be

Cas I'm Cassie.

Mark Cassie. Right. Hi. Nice to meet you.

Cas Hi. Yeah.

Mark We didn't wake you up last night / did we?

Cas No not at all / you must have

Mark Great.

Cas been very quiet.

Mark Cool.

Cas I mean. Coming in.

Mark No I know. Yeah. We did
　try anyway. Bit to drink. You know.

Cas Right.

Mark Sorry to just
　barge in on you I thought

Cas It's fine. Honestly. I'm just
　writing this speech so

Mark Yeah?

Cas for work but. Anyway. It's nice to meet you. I've heard loads about you.

Mark Have you?

Cas Yeah.

Mark Really?

Cas I mean
you know.

Mark I might just
sorry it's just

He means his shirt.

Cas Sorry?

Mark No just

He tugs his shirt out from under her.

Cas Oh! / Sorry

Mark Sorry. No you're alright. Thanks. Just gonna –

He means go to the toilet.

Cas Sure. Cool. Yeah. Go ahead.

He goes towards the kitchen. You have to go through the kitchen to get to the loo.

Mark Unusual layout you've got here, isn't it?

Cas I'm sorry?

Mark Toilet through the kitchen.

Cas Oh right.

Mark Feel like I'm on my gap year!

He joke-shudders.

Cas Oh.

He laughs.
    She sort of laughs.

(Yeah.)

Mark Back in a sec.

    He goes.

Cas OK.

    She shakes her head a little.
        On a whim, she finds a reflective surface and checks her appearance.
        The loo is flushed.
        She sits down and continues tapping.
        Mark re-enters. He is wearing his shirt. He has also wet his hair and washed his face.

Mark So / I was just

Cas Where's Rose? / Oh sorry

Mark No it's /
    you go.

Cas Is it
    I was just saying where's Rose?

Mark Job interview.

Cas Oh good. That's good. What for / did you

Mark I don't know what for.

Cas No OK.

Mark Sounds like she's well qualified for uh just about anything.

Cas Is she?

Mark Done about a thousand jobs! In a good way I mean. I'm sure.

Cas I don't really
she just moved into the flat so

Mark Gumtree. Yeah, she said.

Cas My old flatmates moved back to Portugal to get
married. So

Mark Good for them.

Cas Well. You know.

Mark What is it you do again?

Cas I'm a
I work for a feminist organisation? We uh
I'm an activist, I mainly lobby parliament

Mark Wow.

Cas on their behalf. Wow?

Mark Yeah. Good for you. Didn't know people still did
that kind of thing.

Cas Feminism?

Mark Well. You know. Not
per se. I just think
No. I don't know.

Cas What?

Mark No. It's admirable. It's very
Greenham Common!

Cas Is it?

Mark Isn't it?

Cas You seem to know.

Mark No. Me? I'm in marketing. I know about
you know. A campaign for a new men's razor. Yes.
But uh
waving banners and lying in front of tanks?

Cas Did I say I waved banners? I said I lobby parliament.

Mark Quite right. Parliament. No, that sounds wicked. Good for you. Listen I might just

He means go.

Cas Think feminism is irrelevant do you?

Mark What?

Cas Think we've done it all. Got our equality what we all banging on about that sort of thing?

Mark Not / at all I just

Cas Because the rape conviction rate says otherwise doesn't it?

Mark Does it?

Cas And the murders from domestic violence.

Mark I mean

Cas And international sexual exploitation of vulnerable women. All these things say otherwise don't they?

Mark Hey. No one said it was easy. I just think

Cas What?

Mark This is a bit
you know. Life. Not easy.

Cas Isn't it?

Mark Course not.

Cas Is for you. Isn't it? With your fancy job and your where is it you live? Chiswick?

Mark Might just go and

Cas Oh sorry am I making you uncomfortable?

He goes.

Bet you drive a car don't you? Bet you've got a pension. Bet you've got savings. Bet you've got PLANS FOR THE FUTURE?

Beat.

Wanker.

Beat.

Shit.

Beat.
She looks about despairingly.

Fuck.

Gets up. Goes into the kitchen. Sound of the kettle going on.
Comes back into the living room just as Mark comes back in.

Mark Just going to

Cas Listen, I'm really sorry.

Mark It's

Cas No. I do this
  aggressive thing it's just
  it's not you. Honestly! I'm trying to give up being confrontational about feminism for New Year but the problem *is* you see my other resolution is I'm giving up smoking and that makes me feel really uh
  tense and and
  argumentative and probably I should have done one or the other you know but
  I'm worried about cancer so

Mark OK . . .

Cas I'm boiling the kettle?

Mark I've got / things I should be

Cas Look I'm sorry OK? Please have a cup of tea with me. You're Rose's boyfriend I feel like
  I don't want us to get off on the wrong foot.

Mark I'm

Cas Please?

Mark No I don't mean. I mean tea would be nice it's just
  I'm not Rose's boyfriend.

Cas What?

Mark No I mean. I'm not just some random guy / just

Cas I / was going to say!

Mark wandered in off the street just
  I just mean it's
  early days. You know. Is that what she said?

Cas I probably just
  assumed. She's cool. Rose. She seems cool.

Mark Yeah she's a nice girl. Lots of fun.

Cas Well. She's twenty-seven so

Mark Is she?

Cas Woman. Really.

Mark She told me she was twenty-three.

Cas Oh.

Mark I thought she looked a bit

Cas No she might have

Mark Twenty-seven.

Cas So um what kind of tea would you like?

She goes out to the kitchen.

Mark Oh um. OK. Well. You got any herbal?

Cas (*off*) Think so. Hang on.

Mark Drink less caffeine.

Cas (*off*) What's that?

Mark My New Year's uh . . .

Cassie comes back in.

Cas We've got Earl Grey or rosehip.

Mark Ooooh. OK. Um. Um. Um. Rosehip please.

Cas Giving up caffeine?

She goes out.

Mark This is day
what is it
Four?

He does the Big Brother voice.

Day four. Mark is givin' up caffeine.

He looks around.

Nah it's OK this place. You rent don't you?

Cas (*off*) What's that?

Mark What's your square footage here?

Cassie comes back in.

Cas What did you say?

Mark What's your rent like?

Cas Yeah it's alright. Four hundred a month?

Mark In total?

Cas Each.

Mark whistles.

That's cheap.

Mark Yeah no. Sure. Just
  thinking what I could be making renting my spare
room out.

Cas Right.

Mark Probably even more in Chiswick.

Cas Oh yeah well in Chiswick. I mean. Yeah.

Mark Do you despise me for being a property owner?

Cas Yes.

Mark Are you going to shout at me again?

Cas No.

Mark Go on.

Cas No.

Mark You know you want to.

Cas No. I want to make the tea. Piss off.

  She exits.

Mark Not very women's lib!

  Cassie shouts from the kitchen.

Cas Fuck you! Misogynist!

  He laughs.
    After a second, she comes back.

Did you say Earl Grey or rosehip?

Mark Earl Grey please.

Cas Fine.

  Blackout.

3
VOICES

ten minutes to
eight minutes to
Hammersmith
Gloucester Road
four hundred and thirty
five
three minutes to bus stop
and tube just
you would be sharing with a keen sports player
two girls at the same time
an unlicensed minicab
six months
two couples
four singles
five hundred metres
two minutes
two kiwis

4
MARK'S FLAT

Tim is loafing.
    The front door slams.
    Tim hurries to the computer and tries to look in the middle of things.

Mark (*off*) Muffhead?

Tim In here.

    Mark enters.

Mark Course you are. Where else would you be?

Tim It's my night off.

Mark Yes. I know.

Tim You're late back.

Mark Fucking District Line. Couple of days back in London I want to grab old ladies and *shove* them out the way. Here bitch. Out of my fucking WAY.

He sits. Tim carries on typing.

Mark Onto the tracks! Ha.

Waits for acknowledgement of some kind from Tim.
It doesn't come.
He sighs a little tiny sigh.

What have you done today?

Tim Uh huh. Loads.

Beat.

Mark Such as?

Tim Just sending an email about a job.

Mark Yeah? What kind of job?

Tim The usual.

Mark Muffin!

Tim I know, but this one's really good. It says man *or* woman.

Mark Oh well you're perfect.

Tim No but usually they just want women so I thought I should email.

Mark Leap into action and send an email.

Tim Well.

Mark Did you go to the gym?

Tim I did.

Mark You did? No you didn't.

Tim No I didn't but I rang them.

Mark Did you? What did they say?

Tim It's too expensive.

Mark What?!

Tim It's fifty quid a month. I don't have fifty quid a month.

Mark You don't have fifty quid a month?!

Tim No.

Mark I spend fifty quid a day on nothing!

Tim Well
you're
better than me.

Mark So? Come on, Muffstuff.

Tim What?

Mark What did we talk about?

Tim This is proactive.

Mark What is? Sending pointless emails?

Tim Why are they pointless?

Mark It's like me deciding I want to be a model, Tim. Or no. I mean. It's like it's like
you deciding you want to be a model. You know?

Tim I'm a qualified carer.

Mark How are you?

Tim OK I'm not qualified but I'm experienced. Isn't that more important?

Mark I don't know, is it? Because seems to me like nobody wants you.

Tim I just haven't found the right thing yet.

Mark I'm going to say something brutal now but I want you to know I'm doing it for your own good OK?

Tim OK.

Mark Sure you want me to?

Tim No.

Mark I think you need to hear it.

Tim OK.

Mark When you apply for a job
as a 'carer'
people look at you and think
that guy can't even look after himself.
Why would I want him to look after me?

  Beat.

Tim I think they just want a lady.

Mark What about that woman with the fish fingers?

Tim She didn't care so long as you spoke English.

Mark But she still didn't want you.

Tim I didn't want her. Racist.

Mark Stop making excuses! Look at yourself! OK? Look at what's going on here. Look at me. Come on. Look at me.

  Tim does.

And now look at you.

Tim does.

What do you notice?

Tim Uh

Mark We went to one of the top universities in the country. We left the same year.

Tim It's not a top university.

Mark Course it is. Listen to what I'm saying. We're the same age. And yet what? I make eighty K a year. And what do you make?

Tim Well

Mark Chickenburgers.

Tim I am looking.

Mark Yeah but what for? You have to get real, Tim. Start rolling with the punches a bit yeah? So you think to yourself
   OK the carer thing. Not working out. What can I do instead? Do I have a suit? Do I have an up-to-date CV?

Tim I just

Mark Don't make excuses.

Tim No

Mark Stop making excuses!

Tim I'm not!

Mark You are!

Tim Look, if you want me to go –

Mark I don't want you to go for fuck's sake I said you could live here, I'm trying to help you! OK? I'm not having a go. I'm just saying carry on like this you're going to wake up one morning with fucking

no job. No future. No

nothing except a new species of fungus growing under your big fat man boobs.

Tim What?

Mark When was the last time you had a salad?

Tim It's my night off!

Mark I just

want you to be happy. Right? That's all I'm saying. And I know that's hard at the moment because obviously you're sad and you've had a 'loss' and of course you need time to get over it but Tim

it's January. It's been what

four? five? months? And every night I get home and you're still here and *she's* still here and I just think

when is it going to change?

Tim Christmas was difficult.

Mark Tim. Life is difficult. OK? She wasn't even –

Tim What?

Mark Doesn't matter.

Tim No what?

Mark Mate. Nothing. It doesn't matter.

Pause.

Mark and Tim are in the living room. Two minutes ago they had an argument about Tim being a useless cunt.

Tim tries to summon a laugh.

Fancy a beer?

Tim Yes please.

24

Mark Go on then. You know where they are.

Tim gets up to get the beer.

Fuck I'm knackered.

Tim So uh
  how was last night?

Mark In what way?

Tim Didn't you see whatshername again?

Mark Who? Crazy Rose?

Tim Yeah. Was she? You stayed over though.

Tim exits.

Mark Yeah well. Rude not to. But put it this way, it's lucky we don't have a pet rabbit.

Tim (*off*) You what?

Mark Keeps texting me pictures of herself in her underwear? I'm like
  er . . .

Tim comes back. Two beers.

Tim So you gonna see her again?

Mark Cheers. Not unless she turns up with an ice pick eeh eeh

He does the Psycho *mime.*

Tim Nah. Do you think she will?

Mark No.

They drink their beers.

Why you so interested?

Tim I'm not.

Mark Yes you are.

Tim gets up.

Tim Shall we get a pizza?

Mark Changing the subject.

Tim I'll get the menu.

Mark I'll have a pepperoni please.

Tim exits.
Mark goes to the computer.

Can I close this? I want to Google something.

Tim comes back in, holding the menu.

Tim What did you say?

Mark I need to Google.

Tim Yeah go ahead. Pepperoni did you say?

Mark You know I read this thing the other day:
'If you don't *believe* you're worth a million dollars a year
then you probably aren't.'

Tim . . .

Mark Just think about it. Yeah?

Tim Thanks.

Mark No problem.

Mark is at the computer. Googling.
Tim is going to call for pizza.

Tim So
Pepperoni?

Mark So fucking slow . . .

Tim Mark?

Mark Aha! Gotcha. Cassie . . .
Grey. Ooh. Wicked. She's got a blog!

Mark scrolls down.

Tim You want pepperoni?

Mark No thanks. Chicken and sweetcorn. Extra cheese.

Blackout.

5
CASSIE AND ROSE'S FLAT

Cassie stands, holding a piece of notepaper.

Cas Rape Tube offers you free teen girl rape DVD and
videos. Schoolgirl becomes the star of a gang-rape porn
movie! Cute teen abducted and raped by perverted dude.
Top quality rape porn at Free Rape Porn dot com.
Cruelty Porn dot com, fresh rape porn every day!
Rapescan dot com, your guide to the best and most
brutal rape porn sites! Scream and Cream features the
largest archive of the most violent rape porn ever
produced! Rape Shock dot com: rape porn reviews. Find
out what you get before you join! Girls are raped and
humiliated in the most extreme ways! Only real shocking
rapes. A hundred per cent free!

*Rose enters. She is holding her mobile phone. She
needs something.*

Rose Hi.

Cas Oh hi. Sorry. I'm just

Rose Practising your speech?

Cas Trying to.

Rose I know. Sorry to interrupt. It's just I need to know Cassie: was it the rosehip tea?

Cas The what?

Rose The tea you made Mark. Was it the rosehip?

Cas I don't
maybe?

Rose Did he ask for that specifically?

Cas I don't

Rose And did he drink it?

Cas I
think so. I don't remember.

Rose No, it's OK. It's good.

Cas Is it?

Rose Rose. Rosehip. It has to mean something. That sort / of

Cas Might have been Earl Grey. I don't

Beat.

Rose Earl Grey?

Cas Maybe.

Beat.

Rose And he definitely didn't say anything else?

Cas He came in. We had tea. We chatted about feminism. He left.

Rose Nothing about where he was going or

Cas Nope.

Rose Did / he

Cas That's everything. OK?

Rose I'm just really worried Cassie. I think maybe something terrible's happened.

Cas Oh no. Really? What do you mean?

Cassie finds her nicotine replacement inhaler and takes a drag.

Rose Well why else is he not calling back?

Cas Oh I see. I mean

Rose I had this awful thought that maybe he'd lost his phone. Because if he's lost his phone he's lost my number hasn't he? And how would he ever find me again?

Cas I thought you were friends on Facebook.

Rose Yeah but that's what's weird. His Facebook's disappeared!

Cas OK . . .

Rose What could cause something like that?

Cas Er

Rose Because this is what I'm thinking Cassie. I mean first I thought his phone was just lost. But now I'm thinking
  what if he was mugged? What if he's just
  out there
  bleeding or
  lying in a ditch somewhere and I just feel like

Cas Rose!

Rose What?

Cas OK I'm not
  because maybe you're right you know? I don't know.
I just

I just think isn't there sort of the possibility that maybe he just
   isn't calling you?

Rose Not calling me? Why?

Cas Come on.

Rose What?

Cas Because he's a man?

   Beat.

Rose Cassie
   when we made love
   he looked in my eyes the whole time.

Cas Rose

Rose A man like that doesn't just not call you!

Cas Sometimes they do.

Rose You didn't see the way he looked at me.

Cas I just
   I just think
   you don't know. You don't know what he's thinking.
The only thing / you have

Rose When we first met

Cas That's not the point. I'm not talking about how you met or what happened or what he said I'm talking about the facts. OK? And the fact is
   he hasn't called you and all I'm saying is
   I'm not trying to be harsh but you can't really escape the *fact* that if he wanted to
   don't you think it's reasonable to assume that he could in fact if he really wanted to
   find a way to call you?

Rose You're so right! I should go round there.

Cas What? No! What?

Rose Check if he's OK.

Cas Course he's OK! He's just
    doesn't matter.

Rose You don't know him, Cassie. OK? This isn't
normal.

Cas What are you talking about? *You* don't know him!

Rose I know enough.

Cas Yeah you think that, then one day he turns round
and smacks you in the face or or
    burns your house down and murders your children!

Rose Come on Cassie! You'll never find a man with that
sort of attitude.

Cas Oh my God. No? Well. Maybe I don't want to find
a man.

Rose Ah.

Cas I mean. I don't
    of course I'd like to find
    someone.

Rose A man?

Cas Yes but not just any man. You know? Men
    most men aren't very evolved. Like
  This what you're going through here is a classic
example. All this guy has to do is *communicate* with you.
Be *honest*. Text you. Let you know. But does he? No.
And why?

Rose Ah I see what you mean.

Cas Because

Rose You mean maybe it's an emotional thing? Like

Cas well

Rose for example a fear of how quickly he's falling in love with me?

Cas No! I mean because he's probably
along with ninety-nine per cent of men
for all their gun-toting
wife-beating
warmongering bullshit: a total emotional coward.

Delighted, Rose applauds.

What?

Rose Was that from your speech?

Cas No.

Rose Thought you might be practising.

Cas No, my speech
doesn't matter.

Rose No go on. It sounded good?

Cas No, you're OK.

Rose I can't believe I live with a real life feminist. My mum was so into that whole Germaine Greer Simone de Belle Jour thing. You know? Burning her bra. Sleeping around. Come on. Do me the rest!

Cas Yeah no. Next time maybe.

Rose I thought it was about porno. Because I was going to say to you I know this guy right. American. He was in the gym one day and this guy came up to him and said, 'Hey man you've got a big wanger do you want to be in my movie?' and this guy (the guy I know) what was his name? I think it was Douglas? I might have his number actually if you want it. But anyway he was like, 'Yeah sure' and the next day he was on set literally just having sex with all these women, getting paid thousands of dollars.

Cas Right.

Rose It's his job now. He's loaded.

Cas Wow.

Rose Yeah. Because before that he sold hot dogs.

Beat.

I used to hate hot dogs. That cheap sort of
 Meat. Do you know what I mean?

Cas Yeah.

Rose I was going to come and watch you but I got that job so I won't make it.

Cas You got it?

Rose Yep.

Cas That's great! The karaoke one? / Well done!

Rose Yes. Thanks.

Cas Why didn't you say?

Rose Just forgot.

Cas When do you start?

Rose Tuesday.

Cas And when do you get paid?

Rose I need to check.

Cas It's just
 remember I said about the rent?

Rose The rent?

Cas The standing order for the rent?

Rose Oh right. Yes. Course. How much is it again?

Cas Well. Um. It's
four hundred. Same as the first time. Only I've had to
cancel mine till your money comes into my account and
we can't leave it much longer or Shizad gets upset.

Rose I'll see what I can do.

Cas Well. OK. I mean
you need to kind of sort it out so

Rose Sort it out. See what I can do.

Cas And
um
while we're on the subject
sorry but
these letters came for you

Rose Oh.

Cassie gets up and goes to a shelf.
   *She takes down three brown envelopes and holds
them out to Rose.*

When?

Cas I don't know. They've been on the table downstairs.

Rose looks horrified. Tries not to take them.

Rose How did they find me so quickly?! Honestly. It's
been
what? A month? It's like some kind of evil
dark
magic or

Cas I put your name on the council tax. Maybe

Rose Did you?

Cas And the electoral roll. Sorry.

Rose Shit.

Cas I sort of had to for the bills and also
well there's a local election soon. I thought you
might want me to.

Rose Why?

Cas So you can vote.

Rose What for?

   Beat.

Cas In the local election?

Rose Oh well. Don't worry. It doesn't matter. So long as
you don't reply they can't find you.

Cas They? Who's they?

Rose Well yes. Quite! You never know do you because
they just keep selling it on and on and on until one day
some big guy called Tony rocks up at your front door
and takes your TV away do you know what I mean? And
you think it's a disaster until two days later when the TV
licence man comes round and then it's sort of good cos
you can let him in and say ha ha I don't have a telly any
more ha ha. Or a stereo. Or my nice bookcase.

Cas Oh.

Rose We should go out for a drink or something
shouldn't we? Like get really pissed together or do you
cook much?

Cas Sometimes.

Rose I cook the most delicious meat-free Hungarian
goulash. I'll make it for you one night, have a sit-down.

Cas Yeah? Definitely.

Rose One night next week maybe?

Cas Maybe. / I just
right now I should probably

Rose The trick is to use authentic
what?

Cas Sorry

Rose Hungarian paprika.

Cas Sorry. I just
should probably
get on with it.

Rose Oh. Good. Yes. I'll leave you to it.

Cas Thanks.

Rose Thanks for the chat. I better try Mark again before bed.

Cas OK.

Rose Wish me luck!

Blackout.

6

OUTSIDE THE CONFERENCE CENTRE

Cassie is smoking.
Mark has turned up unexpectedly. He has a copy of
The Female Eunuch *in his coat pocket. Maybe we can't
see it, but it's there.*

Cas This is so fucked up.

Mark What is?

Cas You are. Being here. What do you want?

Mark Cassie

Cas No don't say you want to become a feminist again because I don't believe you.

Mark I didn't –
I said I have become interested in feminism.

Cas Yeah? Well I've become interested in why you're ignoring Rose and at the same time sending me emails!

Mark No I just

Cas What?

Mark because

Cas She's sitting at home telling herself you've been in a car accident and you turn up here with a copy of *The Female Eunuch*. What the fuck is your game?

Mark No game.

Cas OK your
deal your problem

Mark No problem. Just
Listen. Rose and me
we met in a bar. We had a few nights of fun. Pissed as farts. I thought we understood each other and then suddenly she starts calling me all the time. Saying she's in love with me!

Cas Maybe if you replied . . .

Mark She doesn't give me a chance. She calls. An hour later she calls again. I mean
if a bloke did that to you what would you think?

Cas I'd think he was a psycho!

Mark Exactly. See?

Cas I usually err on the side of thinking all men are psychos because men have the power to murder me and dispose of my body and never get caught.

Mark OK.

Cas What are you afraid of?

Mark Nothing.

Cas Apart from the obvious.

Mark What's that?

Cas The truth?

Mark I'm telling the truth!

Cas Which is what?

Mark That I want to learn more about feminism.

Cas I have to go back inside now.

Mark Is it really so hard to believe?

Cas Yes!

Mark Why?

Cas Because!

Mark Because what? You never changed someone's mind before? I thought that's what you did for a living.

Cas What's your point?

Mark My point is maybe you're really good at it.

Beat.

Your speech was incredible.

Cas No it wasn't.

Mark It was fucking sensational.

Cas Ow. Get out. You're hurting my arsehole.

Mark Cassie. Seriously. Please.

Cas What? What? What do you want?

Mark How can you even joke about this, it's like you're deliberately undervaluing yourself or something. Why do you do that? Listen to me, I'm telling you I thought your speech was fantastic.
  I was really moved by it.

Cas Oh yeah? Which bit?

Mark Just all of it really. I think
  you know this idea that
  I think I didn't really understand what it's like to be a girl and have all that
  that stuff all that imagery just constantly bombarding you and making you feel
  you know. Like a sex object basically.

Cas Uh huh.

Mark And the old statistics are pretty shocking. Rape and
  that sort of thing. I didn't know it was that bad.

Cas Yeah? Well. It is.

Mark Yeah. So. You know. I feel
  I'm just really glad I came. I feel like I learned something.

Cas Well.
  OK. I mean. I'm glad of that.

Mark So thank you. OK?

  He smiles.
    She smiles a bit back.

Mark Do you uh
  fancy a quick drink? Talk about it more?

Cas What?

Mark There's a nice pub round the corner.

Cassie laughs.

What?

Cas No OK. Go on.

Mark No. Not in a bad way just
   doesn't have to be a drink. A coffee? An ice lolly?
Anything just
   I'd love to get to know you better.

Cas Fuck you.

Mark What?

Cas No, fuck you Mark.

Mark What did I say?

Cas You know I had this
   this pathetic moment of hope just then that maybe
some bit of my fucking rambling bullshit had managed
to land somewhere it actually made a difference.

Mark And it / did.

Cas And even while you were saying it I was telling
myself not to get my hopes up you know
   don't get your hopes up Cassie it's extremely unlikely
for a a a
   good-looking
   white
   public schoolboy to really give a fuck about any of this
it's much more likely he's just trying to get in your pants.

Mark That's not what this is.

Cas I'm going inside now. OK? Just
   call Rose.

Mark Cassie wait! OK OK I'll call Rose. I promise.

Cas Don't promise. Just do it.

Mark I will and I'm sorry OK? I'm just being an idiot. You inspired me so I wanted to hang out with you but I'm already on the mailing list so I'll just
    you know. Start coming along. See you here. And before you go
    Cassie? I just want to say something. OK? You're right. You're
    you're right about everything. I had an agenda and I had a
    I can't stop thinking about you and I admit that did drive me in coming here today and it was wrong of me not to just come out and say that from the beginning but at the same time you know
    your hope
    it wasn't pathetic. It was real. There is hope. And whether you want to be my friend or not
    you did do something here today. You have changed something. You've changed me.

    Beat.

No matter how impossible it seems to you at this moment in time.

    Beat.

Cas There's a panel talk. Here. On Thursday.

Mark OK.

Cas It's on the newsletter.

Mark Sounds great.

Cas You're free?

Mark Definitely.

Cas I can't make it.

Mark Oh.

Cas But I can email Jessica. Reserve you a ticket.

Mark Sounds perfect. Thank you. Maybe afterwards
I can
    I don't know. Send you an email. Let you know how it
went.

Cas Do what you want.

Mark You don't have to reply.

Cas I won't.

Mark I understand.

Beat.

Cas I do want to believe you.

Mark I know.

Cas I just
    it would be nice to think there's men out there who
care. You know?

Mark We're out there Cassie.

Beat.

We really are.

Blackout.

7
CHEAP 'N' CHICKEN

Tim is behind the counter in his uniform.
Rose has come to find him.

Rose And actually the colour rose has all these mystical
meanings. And it's the colour of one of the chakras. Rose
chakra.

She laughs.

Imagine if that was my name. Rose Chakra. What's your name? I know it's Tim but your second name what's your second name?

Tim Muffin.

Rose No. Tim Muffin?

She looks at him in wonder.

Tim Do you want fries with that?

Rose Yes please. Because you were destined to be . . .

Tim Large?

Rose Well. Tubby maybe.

Tim I meant the fries.

Rose Oh I see. Yes please. No but I just think Muffin. It's like that whole Shakespearean debate you know? Which is particularly relevant to me of course because I always wonder what a rose by any other name would smell like? And I remember at my school there was this boy. John Caves. And when we were thirteen or fourteen maybe we went on this school trip and he swam into this pothole and just never came out. And the whole time I was just like oh my God. I mean

it was like his *destiny*. John . . . Caves. And ever since then I've been really into people's names and what they mean and did you know that if you number all the letters in the alphabet from one to nine and then add up all the letters in your name according to where they come in the alphabet and combine that with the date of your birth then you can actually generate information not only about your personality but about the entire span of your future? I mean people don't think about this shit when they have babies they just think oh let's call him

Neil or whatever but that name is going to
well, you're shaped by it in a way because
aside from the numerological implications the very
sound or feel of the name *Neil* is also going to affect how
people are going to treat you and actually if you'd been
called something totally different like
Brutus
then maybe you would have actually
been a different person. I mean. Isn't that so fucked up?!

Tim I haven't always been fat.

Rose No? When did it happen?

Tim I mean. I guess
when my Nan got ill?

Rose Oh yeah Mark said she died.

Tim Yeah.

Rose Of lung cancer? Did she smoke?

Tim Loads.

Rose Did you love her very much?

Tim Yes.

Rose Was it very sad?

    Beat.

Tim Yeah.

Rose Poor Timmy Muffin.

    He looks at her.

What?

Tim I don't believe in destiny.

Rose What? Do you believe in God?

Tim No way.

Rose The devil?

Tim I don't think so.

Rose What do you believe in?

Tim I believe in – /
I believe in –

Rose I believe in
Fairies gnomes elves cyclopses
Leprechauns unicorns
Pixies witches wizards
angels dwarves
True love
Love at first sight
and the lost city of Atlantis.

  A bell rings.

Tim Dwarves?

Rose Yup.

Tim How can you / not –?

Rose And do you know why?

Tim Your food –

Rose I'm telling you something. Do you know why?

Tim Why what?

Rose Why I know those things exist? Because when I was a little girl I went into a field one day
a sunny day
I went into a field and I looked up at the sky
this beautiful azure sky and I said
Fairies?
If you're out there?

45

Give me a sign! Any sign!
Just tell me you're there!
And I shut my eyes tight and I could hear this music
suddenly this beautiful music like harps or something like
that and when I opened my eyes I was surrounded by
hundreds of those daffodil heads. You know? The clocks.
Floating past me. Hundreds of them. So beautiful. And
from that moment on I've been a believer.

Tim Dandelions.

Rose What?

Tim The clocks. They're dandelions / not

Rose What did I say?

Tim Daffodils. You said / daffodils.

Rose No I didn't. Dandelions. Don-de-lion. Lion's tooth.
That's what that means. I was surrounded by hundreds of
lions' teeth!

Tim Ha. I like that.

Rose Yeah? I think it's important to try and believe in
something Tim. You know? Especially these days.

Tim Do you want

Beat.

Rose What?

A bell rings.

Tim No I just. Best (get that).

He goes to fetch the food.
Rose psychs herself up.

Rose Come on Rose . . .

She reaches into the air and grabs an imaginary
opportunity.

Tim comes back.

Tim I think I stopped believing because
   when Nan died I realised for the first time that when
you die
   that's it. You die. You're gone. And you aren't ever
   ever
   coming
   back. Deluxe veggieburger with cheese and a large fries
do you want sauce with that?

Rose No thanks.

Tim Three seventy-nine.

Rose You're going to charge me?

Tim Oh. Sorry.

Rose It is a wise man knows any run of luck whether
good or bad will come to an end.

Tim Uh huh?

Rose Did you know I've got a job as a karaoke hostess?
In that bar on the High Road.

Tim I didn't know that!

Rose My run of bad luck has come to an end, Tim. I still
believe that. And I feel
   today
   as though I've found in you a kindred spirit. Do you
know what that means?

Tim I think so.

Rose It surprises me because I'd never usually be friends
with someone with so much blood on their hands but I
get the feeling this isn't your dream job am I right?

Tim Yes.

Rose Then fine.

Tim I don't know what Mark told you but I'm actually in the er

proceeds of pursuing a career in health care?

Rose Really? That's so amazing! It's funny because I was a bit nervous about coming. You never know in these situations if people are going to take sides do you know what I mean?

Tim What

sorry. Situations?

Rose Well. Break-ups. I mean. Poor Mark. Imagine thinking I'd be better off without him!

Tim Oh.

Rose If I'm honest when he called me I felt really rejected you know? But then yesterday I was walking down Oxford Street and I saw a *cornflower-blue dress* in the window of Selfridges?

He doesn't understand.

Mark's favourite colour?

Tim Oh.

Rose And it was like the universe was screaming at me you know. Stop wallowing! You can't just give up like this! You're a twenty-seven-year-old woman! Time is running out! And not just for me. For all of us. You know they say the world might end in two years, Tim. We can't keep worrying about what-ifs. We must live every day like it's our last! Seize the moment!

Tim Can I have your phone number?

Rose Yes Tim! What?

Tim No I just thought

maybe as kindred spirits? we should exchange numbers.

Rose Numbers! Yes! Perfect!

She extracts from somewhere an eyeliner and writes down her number for him.

Rose You know what this is Timmy? It's the influence of Uranus.

Tim Oh yeah?

Rose I said to myself on my way here: the only thing standing between me and true love is the sum of three hundred and ninety-nine pounds
   or the security guard at Selfridges
   and
Mark's flatmate. And now you're already on my side. Isn't that amazing? It's like
   all you have to do is *ask*!

Tim Right.

Rose So this is my number. What I need you to do is talk to Mark. Find out when he'll be in. Text me. And once I've got the dress I'll be able to come over. Right?

Tim You want
   sorry. You want to come over?

Rose Tim! Keep up! I need you to let me into the flat, OK? So I can talk to Mark face to face. And in the meantime, be on the look out for signs. OK? Colours. Numbers. Meteors. Road signs. Anything which might mean something. Right?

Tim Thing is

Rose Is there a problem?

Tim No. No it's just

Rose What?

Tim I mean if I let you in
    you're not going to stab him or / something?

Rose Tim!

Tim No I know I just
    what if he doesn't change his mind?

Rose If I promise not to stab him will you let me in?

Tim Yeah course.

Rose I promise not to stab Mark.

Tim Right. I mean
    OK then.

Rose Is that a yes?

Tim Yes.

Rose Yes! I love you!

    Blackout.

8

VOICES

I want
average
Asian
articulate
adventurous
eating in
eating out
staying in
going out
a sense of humour is a must
trust

honest
clean
pigeons
random acts of kindness
a good bottle of
white men
no husbands
no expectations
no mind games
jeans and a T-shirt and
likes sucking cock
must be compassionate
honest
reliable
flexible
sexual
brutal
central
Jubilee and
District and
Circle ads
smalls ads
mind the gap
small fries
big baps
no pics
no reply
no answer
no father
no baggage
left unattended will be treated as suspicious

9

MARK'S FLAT

Cassie has arrived at Mark's flat.
  He is in the kitchen.
  She looks nice.

Cas Isn't she amazing though? It's just so nice to hear
someone talk with that kind of seventies
  conviction you know? I feel like I never hear those
voices any more. Just
  unapologetically political or
  you know?

  *He emerges with wine. He is wearing a T-shirt with a
  feminist slogan on it.*

Mark If I'm completely honest I didn't get everything she
said.

Cas Yeah I know what you mean.

Mark Like some of it went over my head.

Cas Me too! But it's like
  you don't care because
  it's more just how she says it? Like
  from before the days when we had to be embarrassed or

Mark Yeah.

Cas pretend it doesn't matter any more. You know?

Mark Is red OK?

Cas Perfect.

  *He sets about opening it. When it is open he pours it
  into two glasses.*

Cas Swanky flat.

Mark Yeah?

Cas Where's your flatmate?

Mark Working.

Cas What does he do?

Mark He's in investment. In the city?

Cas I knew you'd have a flat like this. What colour would you call this? Sort of eggshell is it?

Mark It's environmentally friendly emission-free clay-based paint. I believe the shade is called 'fresh air'. Here you go.

Cas Thanks. And what's this thing here?

Mark Oh it's just Tim's granny's ash tray.

Cas Kooky.

Mark Yeah. Cheers.

Cas Cheers.

Mark To an equal society!

Cas Mark. It's OK. We can just drink to I don't know friendship or something.

Mark To friendship.

They clink glasses.

How's Rose?

Cassie groans.

Cas Oh God.

Mark That bad?

Cas Not about you. The rent.

Mark She still hasn't paid?

Cas No I fucking paid in the end. On my credit card. I made her *promise* to pay me back.

Mark And?

Cas She says she doesn't have it and the thing is it's due again in less than a week and it comes out of my account and if she doesn't get the money then I'm just completely fucked.

Mark Can't you kick her out?

Cas Can I tell you something?

Mark OK.

Cas You have to promise not to tell anyone.

Mark Promise.

Cas The police called.

Mark What?

Cas Apparently
the guy she lived with before
some money went missing. Something about a cheque book?

Mark No way. What did you say to them?

Cas I didn't know what to say. I just said she wasn't in at the moment they'd have to call back.

Mark Shit. You need to say something.

Cas I just
something about her
I know this is a stupid thing to say but something about her scares me. You just
I don't know her. You know? I got her off Gumtree.

Mark Remember how she was with me?

Cas I know. I think that now.

Mark Out of nowhere just

Cas Shit.

Mark You know she told me once her dad was a mass murderer.

Cas What? Did she say that?

Mark Among other things.

Cas Who did he murder?

Mark I didn't ask.

Cas Why not?

Mark Dunno.

They giggle.

Cas Poor Rose.

Mark Poor me!

Cas I know but I feel bad for her.

Mark Why?

Cas Because
I'm here?

Mark Having a drink with a feminist mate? What's wrong with that?

Cas I know, I just

Beat.

Mark I'm really glad you agreed to come back.

Cas Me too. It's nice.

Mark There's
something I want to say to you.

Cas Oh. Uh
Can't we just

Mark Not
really.

Cas OK.

Cassie starts looking for her cigarettes.

Mark I think I need to say it because I think if I don't say it then I will have been dishonest. And I don't want to be dishonest with you Cassie.

Cas OK.

Mark The thing is

Cas Can I smoke in here? Sorry, I just
don't look at me like that I can't help it.

Mark Go ahead.

She lights up.

Cas Thanks. Sorry. There's something you want to say.

Mark Yes. I just
I just wanted to say
I know I'm

Beat.

Cas Go on.

Mark No it's just, it's difficult. Because I guess
What I wanted to say is
I'm a man.

Cas is planning to use the cat as an ashtray.

Cas Yes. What do I do with / this do I –

Mark Just take the head off I
  Yeah like that.

Cas It's a bit full should I empty it?

Mark Nah just
  best not just
  There we go.

Cas Cool. Thanks. Sorry go on what were you saying?
You're a man.

Mark Yes, I am.

Cas You are.

  He takes her hand.

Mark

Mark No it's OK, I'm just
  I'm a man. And these days it's
  It can be hard to know what that means. You know?
I mean I think sometimes about men in my grandfather's
time. Or men the men you see on telly with the guns and
the cause and the
  The passion. I look at those men and I think yeah. You
  You're men. You know?

Cas Terrorists?

Mark No – just
  Men who
  Brave men. Heroes.

Cas Why do you have to kill people to be a hero?

Mark I don't know. You just do.

Cas What?

Mark No you're missing the point. Let me finish, the
point is

I want to be brave Cassie. Fight for what I believe in.
Take action. And I told myself I had two choices: I could
stay afraid and keep quiet or
    be brave and tell you

Beat.

Cas Yes?

Mark that I've been falling in love with you ever since
I first saw you.

Cas Oh.

Beat.

OK.

Mark And I keep waiting for it to stop but instead I just
I just keep falling.

Cas Oh. I see.

Beat.

Mark Are you pissed off?

Cas I don't know.

Mark I understand if you are.

Cas I'm not.

Mark You're not?

Cas I just

Mark I've had an idea.

Cas Mark

Mark This is going to sound silly but I'm just going to
say it anyway because fuck it. OK? Maybe this evening
we could play a game. OK?

She takes her hand away.

58

Cas What about Rose?

Mark Shhhh. Forget that for a second, I want to play a game. You up for it? We're going to pretend

He takes her hand again.

there are no men. And there are no women. And there is no – no – issues or
  history. Herstory. We've never been hurt before or
  we have no reason to doubt each other. There's no other parties involved. No flatmates or colleagues or ex-boyfriends or anyone. Just you. And me.

He catches sight of the cat and is momentarily distracted.

Alone. And we can sit and chat and pretend we're just two human beings who kind of think they might
  like
each other . . .?

Beat.

Who kind of know they might like each other.

Cassie nods.

I want to
  Can I
  Would it be OK if I kissed you now?

Beat.

Cas OK.

Mark OK?

Cas OK.

Mark OK.

Cas OK.

Mark OK?

Cas Hang on, my fag –

She drops it in the urn.

Wait wait

She drinks some wine.

OK.

Mark OK?

Cas OK.

He kisses her.
They snog etc.
Fade.

10

TIM ROBS THE CHEAP 'N' CHICKEN

*Tim is turning out the main lights. Locking the door. He
puts his headphones in. A love song plays so we can all
hear it.*

He dances along. He is very happy.

*He takes a wad of cash out of the till and lays it on the
counter.*

Puts on his coat.

Sticks the money in his pocket.

Blackout.

As before. Fewer clothes.
  A long and uncomfortable pause.
  Cassie is smoking into the cat again.

Cas The phallus is not solely responsible for the act of sex Mark so don't take my power away, OK?

  Beat.

Anyway. You know. It happens. It's nothing to feel bad about.

Mark I don't feel bad.

Cas Oh.

  Beat.

What then?

Mark I feel
  angry.

Cas With me?

Mark No.

Cas Oh?

Mark With the patriarchy.

Cas Oh.

Mark I can't
  Help what I
  I can't help
  I mean
  Look Cassie
  This isn't *Europe*. And it's like you say, the media
  they made me this way. I can't help what I fancy and

I just
     it's like
     down there and
     under here? I never
     I just can't. I mean:
     you're like
     you're like a man.

Cas I'm like
     a woman.

Mark I'm sorry. I know.

     Beat.

I just can't help what turns me on.

     Cassie gets up.
       Beat.

Cassie?

     Pause.

Cas I see.

Mark Do you?

     Pause.
       She drops the fag in the cat.

Cas It's a question I ask myself.

Mark What is?

Cas About what we want and things and and how how
how do you know the difference?

Mark Is it?

Cas Because supposing you were let's say to pick a
random example
     a feminist and you spent your whole life fighting the
the normalisation of pornographic material and and
     you believe in gender equality not just as an ideal but

as a *necessity* and then at the same time you find yourself
    in a completely different sense and or
    context
    wanting to be dominated in the bedroom. For example.
You know? You'd start asking yourself wouldn't you?
Why do I want that? Because
    obviously the most likely explanation is I've been
programmed and
    fed and
    raised on those kinds of ideals which are obviously
difficult to escape but at the same time I manage it with
all these other things so so
    what if it's just inside me? This thing which I want
which so completely
    betrays everything I really believe and makes me some
kind of a
    deviant. Essentially.

Mark Do you want that?

Cas A pervert. What?

Mark Do you want to be dominated?

   Beat.

Cas Maybe?

   Beat.

Mark Oh.

Cas No. I don't
    I don't
    Want that. I don't want to want that. I'm a feminist
I want
    Equality. I want
    Respect I want
    I want to want you to treat me like an equal human
being but

I don't know. At the same time I just
I just want

Mark When you talk about your work. You know the –
The porn stuff. When you gave your speech and

Cas Yeah?

Mark All that talk of dirty fucking.

Cas Yeah?

Mark Turns me on.

Cas Does it?

Mark Yeah.

Cassie stares at him. There is a pause.

Go into the bathroom. There's a razor on the side and
some foam. I want you to shave. Everything. Don't be
careful. Don't take ages. Just do it.

Beat.

I'll be waiting for you in the bedroom.
And when you get there
I'm going to fuck you.

Beat.

Cas I just

Mark Don't talk.

Cas I'm not

Mark Cassie.

Cas Don't

Mark What? You said that's what you wanted, I'm
giving you what you want. Come here.

Beat.

Come here.
  Come on!

She walks towards him.

Cas I don't want to.

Mark Yes you do.

Cas I

Mark Yes you fucking do.

He grabs her arms. She looks at him.
He nods.
She kisses him. They snog. It is very loving.
She turns and goes towards the bathroom. He slaps
her arse. Cassie hesitates. Then carries on.
Mark smiles.
Blackout.

12
VOICES

  sense of humour
  perfect job
  preferably female
  friendly female
  for professional female
  sixteen thousand
  seven-fifty
  one in three
  ten to seven
  seven-seventy
  five days
  no bonus
  modern cheery
  bright cheery fun

large kitchen
well hung
ample storage
spacious
ladies only
huge erection
bright and
light filled
Sky
Sky Plus
DVD
DVD TV
five kiwis
blender
cooker
cleaner
buses
the right candidate will need to be broad-minded
broad-shouldered
with internet broadband
I'm seeking
experienced and confident
competent
confident
someone who
healthy males for
young girls naked
pussy
sixteen
pussy
someone
women and children and
ladies raped and
tortured artist seeks
someone special for a long-term
trial

who knows how to
experiment
who can plan for
men aged between twenty-five and forty
I want
good times
I want
bad times
I want
fourteen
fifteen
someone
I want
someone
to do
to let
to buy
to get
pants
unseen
socks
unheard
a wig
last known
a dress
underground
over
ground almonds
two eggs
baked potatoes
white wine
nights in on our own with
no black men
no Arabs
no fat men
no dramas

no baggage
excuse me
no thank you
can I help you?
over there
over here
can you help me?

13
CASSIE AND ROSE'S FLAT

*Cassie enters the living room as from the bedroom. She
sits as before, working on her laptop. She looks for
something. Can't find it. Gets up. Leaves towards the
bedroom.*

*After a moment, Rose enters, sneaky. She looks
fabulous in a cornflower-blue dress and red stiletto heels.
She totters quickly towards the kitchen. Exits.*

Cassie comes back and sits down.

She checks her emails.

Nothing.

She sighs.

She looks at her mobile phone.

Nothing.

She goes back to her computer.

Quickly, she looks at her phone again.

She thinks about making a call.

She nearly does.

She doesn't.

The loo is flushed.

She looks towards the kitchen.

Beat.

Cas Rose?

Cassie takes a deep breath.

Right.

She stands.
  Rose emerges, hurrying.

Oh!

Rose stops dead. Caught.

Hi.

Rose Hi.

Cas We need to talk. Have you been avoiding me?

Rose Look Cassie I'd love to stop but I've got a cab
coming in five minutes / so

Cas A cab? I thought you didn't have any money.

Rose I'll explain later.

Cas Where are you going?

Rose Just somewhere.

Cas Nice dress.

Rose Yes look I know what you're thinking but the
thing is
  a miracle happened. I needed this dress and I couldn't
afford it and then on Saturday
  at work

Cas What?

Rose I got this envelope with my name on and no listen
to this in it was contained:
  the exact amount of the price of the dress.

Cas What do you mean you needed it?

Rose I mean it's a matter of extreme importance to my
entire future OK so don't have a go at me about money.

Cas Don't have a go at you? The rent's due again on Friday!

Rose I know Cassie but I couldn't use it for rent that money was for the dress. It was a gift from the *universe*. Spend that on rent it's like

Cas Argh!

Rose it's like snubbing the Buddha!

Cas I need that money!

Rose Well I need this dress! Right? It's the dress for the final scene! The dress to walk down stairs in so he sees me across a crowded room and realises he's in / love with me.

Cas What are you talking about?

Rose Cassie, what's rule number one when someone dumps you? You lose weight. Get a fabulous dress and then bump into them unexpectedly so they know they fucked up
   i.e.

She indicates herself.

Cas I need it! Do you get it? I need that fucking money!

Rose OK Cassie listen I don't have it now but I'm ninety-nine point nine per cent certain that after tonight I'm going to have a very rich boyfriend again so as soon as things are up and running I'll ask Mark for a bit of a loan. I'm sure he won't mind.

Cas Mark?

Rose Do you think I look OK?

Cas Which Mark?

Rose Cassie! Mark who I'm in love with! Which Mark!!

Cas You're seeing Mark? When are you seeing him? Where?

Rose Round his house.

Cas You've
    got a date?

Rose No! Silly. I said unexpectedly.

Cas How are you going to bump into him unexpectedly round his house?

Rose Tim's going to let me in.

Cas Tim?

Rose His flatmate. Why do you say it like that?

Cas I don't know. I just
    I'm surprised

Rose Why?

Cas I'm confused. I thought
    I just didn't think you were still
    you know.

Rose What?

Cas What are you doing?

Rose I'm winning Mark back! It's the most important night of my life! Why are you surrounding me with negative energy?

Cas You met him in a pub. You got pissed. You had a few nights of drunken
    meaningless
    it was just sex. It doesn't make him a bad person it just means for him
    you
    he didn't feel the same way.

Rose Who said we were pissed?

Cas You did.

Rose No I never. We met in a vegetarian cafe.

Cas What?
  When?

Rose Before Christmas!

Cas But I thought

Rose I kept trying to tell you how amazing he is but you didn't want to listen!

Cas No I did I just thought

Rose Well you're wrong. A pub! Ha! Me and Mark have the most amazing *how we met* story ever. I was having a falafel and he was on a nearby table and I started telling him about numerology and he was really interested. And then we made friends on Facebook and he sent me this message saying how he'd Googled it and actually it's totally amazing like
  Just stuff he'd never thought about before and didn't realise was out there? And he said

  She laughs.

I want you to come out with me. Have a drink. An ice lolly. He said I want to get to know you better. So we went out and I held out you know? I mean I fancied him loads so I wanted to make him wait. But then he said he had something important to tell me

Cas I don't

  During the following Cassie crumples, slowly. As though something has just collapsed inside her.

Rose and he invited me round to his flat. Amazing. And he'd looked up our numbers? He'd actually looked up our numbers online which I'd already done of course but I hadn't told him and he said we're eighty-eight per cent compatible. Which are pretty good odds, he said. And

he said

listen he said

I've been falling in love with you ever since I first saw you. And I just keep falling. And I know we've both been hurt before but I was wondering if tonight we could play a game. Pretend it's just you and me and we're two human beings who think they might

know they might

like each other.

Beat.

And then he kissed me. Isn't that the most beautiful thing you've ever heard?

Absently, Cassie itches her pubes.

Come on Cassie! Don't look so bitter! Honestly! This doesn't end the way you think.

Cas What?

Rose You think I'm going to get hurt and end up all tragic. Or maybe you don't. Maybe you're worried about the opposite. Maybe you're actually jealous of my potential happiness.

Cassie laughs.

Cas I'm what?

Rose It's like if it works out for me and Mark then somehow it fucks up your philosophy that all men are bastards. You know? You have to start being a bit more optimistic. If you go round telling yourself men are shit all the time then

then you're going to meet a whole load of shit men to prove it.

Cas I don't need to / *tell* myself.

Rose It's bringing me down. God.

Cas Bringing you down?

Rose Yes.

Cas I'm bringing you down?

Rose If I'm being honest. Yes.

Cas Oh you know what? Go on then. Go to Mark's. See what he says. Just don't come crying to me when it all goes wrong OK because I can't listen to it any more. Just waltzing round like a *child* believing in magic and fairydust thinking some fantastical solution will / come along and

Rose Are you talking about me?

Cas fix everything yes I'm talking about you. Life is hard. And unfair. And difficult. And we're on our own here. Right? / No one is going to make it better.

Rose Negative energy!

Rose holds up her hands to make a shield from the negative energy. Covers her head.

Cas Not Mark. Not God. Not Jesus. No man. No one. And until you accept that fact you're just going to keep getting disappointed and let down and hurt. Over and over again and you keep going back for more every time thinking it's different and it never is is it? It never fucking is. So just grow up, OK?

Rose Are you finished?

Cas Grow the fuck up.

Rose retracts the shield.

Rose Right. I have to go. Wish me luck.

Cas No.

Rose I need to go!

Cas No!

Rose Cassie let go of me!

Cas No! You're not going!

Rose Get off!

Cas I won't let / you go!

Rose Get the fuck

> *Rose smacks Cassie in the face.*
> *Cassie cries out. Stumbles backwards.*

. . . off me . . .

> *Beat.*

Now listen before you start making a fuss.

> *During the following, Cassie starts to cry: slow, silent tears.*

I'm sorry I hit you but you were hysterical and I needed to do something. OK? I know you think you're doing the right thing by trying to stop me and I do believe we're kindred spirits or at least we could be maybe one day but sometimes you get very eaten up by negativity and and cynicism and if I let you infiltrate my boundaries then you could be very damaging Cassie. OK? Sometimes things are all or nothing and this is all. It has to be all and you're always trying to tell me it's nothing and it's not nothing. Right? It's never been nothing. It's something. It's something I believe in and I'm passionate about and I would have thought you of all people would understand

that. Right? You're amazing with the things you care about. So strong and
fiery. You fight and you fight and you never give up and I admire you. See? And I just want

I want

I'm going to go out there and I'm going to make things happen. Because I know if I believe it hard enough then Mark

will

love me. And I want you to be proud of me. Because look at me! I'm taking a stand. I'm refusing to submit! I'm being a feminist!

Blackout.

14
VOICES

young professional
must speak English
someone clean
preferably female
English-speaking
English
English
Russian babes and
teenage chicks
we are all human and equal
spunk
a social jungle
cum
go
come
stay
cum

you are free to leave whenever you want
one month's notice
please contact
please call
please
please read the whole advert before calling
life is too short to waste your time on

15
MARK'S FLAT

The front door slams.

Mark (*off*) Muffhead?

  Mark enters.

Fucking District Line was
  Muff-diver?
  Tim?

  Mark is taken aback.
    He looks around.
    He sniffs the air. Something is cooking in the kitchen.
    Tim emerges from his room. He looks smart.

Tim You're back!

Mark Hello.

Tim Thought you were out tonight.

Mark Meeting finished late. I couldn't be fucked. Are you wearing cologne?

Tim No.

Mark What's going on? Are you *cooking*?

Tim I thought you were going out.

Mark Well I'm not am I? I'm here. What the fuck is going on? Why are you dressed up?

Tim I'm not.

Mark Why you so keen for me to go out?

Tim I'm not.

Mark Yes you are.

Tim I'm not I just thought you were.

Mark What are you up to? Tell me.

Tim No.

Mark Aha! So you are up to something.

Tim No.

Mark Yes you are. Tell me!

Tim No.

Mark It's my house!

Tim So?

Mark So I've got a right to know what's going on.

Tim Nothing's going on I just
  I thought I had the place to myself so I was just I thought I'd do some
    pampering.

  Mark snorts. He looks at Tim. Tim squirms. Mark frowns.

Mark You've got someone coming.

  Tim looks somewhere else.

Who is it?

Tim I can't tell you but please
  is there any chance at all you maybe could go out just for a bit?

Mark No way I'm not missing this. Who is it?

Tim No one.

Mark Have to stay and find out then.

Mark sits down.

Tim No! Please
  just for a bit. Just

Mark Who is it?

Tim I can't tell you.

Mark Why not?

Tim I just

Mark Is it a bloke?

Tim No!

Mark It is isn't it!

Tim It's not a bloke it's just

Mark Ah well it was only a matter of time. Don't worry Muffstuff. I don't judge you. I am however somewhat tired and am now ready for my beer.

Tim No.

Mark No? I'm thirsty!

Tim An hour. Half an hour. Just give me half an hour.

Mark Tell me who it is.

Tim I can't. Please Mark. Half an hour.

Mark What do you mean you can't? This is my home, Timothy. I live here. I've been at work all day. I'm tired. I'm thirsty. If you needed me to be out you could have asked but you didn't. I'm not being thrown out of my own home because you're too childish to tell me what's going on in your life right? You want secrets. Fine. But don't expect co-operation.

Tim I'm sorry. I didn't
I thought you'd be out. I didn't think. It won't happen again it's just
I'll tell you after. Right? When I know how it's gone. I just can't tell you now.

Mark Why
not?

Tim I just can't.

Mark Then you pay the price.

Mark smiles. Tim gives up. He goes off towards his bedroom then changes his mind. Returns with gusto.

Tim I'll give you all my DVDs.

Mark No thanks.

The doorbell rings.
Mark jumps up. They run for the door.

I'll get it!

Tim (*overlapping*) I'll go!

Tim manages to get in front of Mark. He pushes him out of the way. Maybe Mark gets accidentally hurt.

Mark Oi!

Tim I said I'll go.

Tim goes.

Mark Fucking
watch yourself mate. Fucking wanker.

Beat.

What the fuck?

Beat.

Never seen you run so fast.

> *Mark stands, hands on hips, waiting for whatever is coming.*
>> *There is a pause.*
>> *Mark shakes his head. Laughs to himself.*

Mark Who is it Tim?
Invite them in!
Don't be shy!

> *Rose enters.*
>> *Tim loiters behind. He is holding Rose's coat.*

Oh.

Rose Hi.

Mark Hi.

> *Mark looks at Tim.*

Rose Remember me?

Mark You cheeky bastard!

> *Tim shrugs.*

Rose It's not his fault.

Mark What isn't?

Rose I made him do it.

Tim Rose

Mark Do what?

> *Rose turns to Tim.*

Rose Timmy?
Could you . . .
I just need a few minutes with Mark.

Mark Oh no!

Rose and Tim look at Mark then turn to each other.

Tim I made a vegetarian lasagne.

Mark laughs really loud. After a second, Rose joins in.

Rose Maybe later. OK?

Tim I just thought

Mark He thought I was going to be out.

Rose What?

Tim No I didn't.

Mark Yes you did.

Rose Please Tim?

Tim Can I come back in a bit?

Rose Course you can, I just need to speak to Mark. Remember?

Tim Yeah.

Rose Thank you.

Tim It's just
all I was thinking was
I'm just not sure it's such a good idea.

Mark What isn't?

Rose How do I look?

Mark What's not a good idea?

Tim You look
amazing.

Rose Well then. Go on.

Tim heads for his room.

Mark Tim. What have you done?

Tim looks at him.

What are you doing?

Tim exits.
   Rose and Mark look at each other.
   She smiles, she is full of love for him.

Rose It's nice to see you.

Mark Is it? What have you done? What's going on?

Rose I'm just on my way to work. Thought I'd pop in.
I work in that karaoke bar on the High Road. I left you
a message.
   You should come down.

Mark I don't really like karaoke.

Rose You don't have to sing.

Mark What do you want?

Rose Do you like my dress?

Beat.

I got it for you.

Mark You shouldn't have.

Rose I've got a surprise for you.

Mark No thanks.

Rose You have to sit down.

Mark I don't want to sit down.

Rose You have to.

Mark I don't have to do anything.

Rose Please Mark. Sit down. If you let me give you my
surprise

I promise
if you still want me to
I'll go. You won't see me ever again.

Mark takes a deep breath.
Exhales.

Mark Fine.

He sits down.
She kneels in front of him.

Rose Shut your eyes.

Mark No!

Rose You have to!

Mark Fuck's sake.

Rose Properly.

Mark It is properly.

Rose You can't see?

Mark No.

Rose OK.

She leans in. Unzips his fly.

Mark What are you doing?

Rose This is the surprise.

Mark What is?

Rose Oh come on Mark. What did you think it was? I
want to
   you know.

She goes for his cock.

Mark No!

Holds back her hand.

Rose Why not?

Mark What did I say to you?

Rose I know what you said. I just think you're wrong
that's all.

Mark Well I don't think I am.

Rose Which is what I want to show you.

Mark Not like this.

Rose How else then?

Mark You can't.

Rose I think I can.

Mark Rose –

She manages to get her hand on his cock.

Rose What's wrong with you Mark?
Don't I look sexy?
On my knees in front of you?
Isn't this what you want?
Oh! I think it is . . .

His cock is getting hard.

Mark It's not that.

Rose *Hard* day at the office
get home
blonde girl comes round offers to *suck* your *cock* for
you and what?
You're going to say no?

She laughs.

Are you going to say no?
What's wrong with you?

Mark Nothing!

Rose Then what's the problem?

Mark I just

Rose Eh?

She moves her face in.

Mark Hey Tim!

Rose Don't!

Mark (*to Tim*) I think you should get out here!

Rose No Tim! Don't come in!

Mark Last chance mate! I think you want to stop this!

Rose No wait!

Mark Last chance!

Rose Tim you promised! If you come out here I'll never speak to you again!

They wait a moment.
Tim doesn't come.

Mark Go on then.

She takes his dick out. Starts sucking it.

Oh God –
fuck

It seems to go on for an uncomfortably long time.
At last, with a small grunt, Mark comes. Rose sits back. She looks at him, makes a big point of swallowing.
A long pause.
Mark does up his trousers. Rose climbs onto his knee and hugs him.
Tries to kiss him.

Ew

He moves his head away.

Rose Oh sorry.

She chuckles.

I like it. Tastes of you. And before you say anything I just want to say thank you. For giving me another chance.

Mark Rose

Rose No listen to me. Don't say anything OK? You never gave me a chance to explain last time. I fucked up before OK I know I did. For some reason I wasn't exactly what you wanted or I let you down or
   I did something anyway that wasn't quite right. But whatever it is you want, I can be that Mark OK? Just tell me what you want.

Mark That was

Rose Eighty-eight per cent remember?

Mark Thing is

Rose I love you.

He sighs.

Mark Rose
   Shit. I don't know how to say this.

Rose Just
   say it. Whatever it is, it's fine. You don't need to be afraid any more.

Mark I'm seeing someone. Else.

Beat.

Another girl. Sorry. I should have said
   before.

Beat.

Rose Oh.

She gets off him. Bends double.

I see.

Mark Are you – ?

She is sick. It is mainly come.

Oh shit. What the
    What are you
    shit
    sorry I'm not
    oh Jesus. Are you
    Sit down. Here sit
    sit down.

Rose Fuck.

Mark Hang on I'll get a
    hold on.

He exits.
    Rose stares.
    He comes back with a cloth. It's kind of useless. He loiters near the sick but can't touch it.

Sorry do you
    I might
    can you

Rose Oh.

She takes the cloth and starts to wipe.

Mark It makes me (gag) just

She cleans.

Fuck.

There is a small pause.
  She finishes cleaning.

Rose We could have an affair. If you wanted. Or
  I mean I don't mind sharing. What do you think about
an open relationship? A threesome?

Mark I'm in love with her.

Rose Oh.

  Beat.

Mark I'm gonna jump in the shower. But you
  I mean. Stay for a bit. Tim can
  lasagne. If you want. Make sure you're
  You know. Better. And

Rose Can you just

Mark What?

Rose Say something?

Mark I don't
  there isn't
  I don't really have anything to say I'm just
  that's it. Really.

Rose Mark

  She grabs his hand.

Please.

Mark Please don't.

Rose I need you.

Mark It's just
  Rose. You don't need me.

Rose I do. I have nothing without you.

Mark Well

He gets her off him. This has gone on long enough.

I don't want you to need me. OK? Get
   I don't even know you. Off. I think
   I think you need help. Right?
   I'm sorry.

   Mark exits to the bathroom.
      Rose gets up off the floor.
      She shuts her eyes.
      She opens her eyes.
      Tim comes back in.
      He looks at her.

Tim Howdit go?

   Beat.

Does he love you again?

Rose He said I need help.

Tim Why?

Rose I'm not sure. I think
   maybe he still cares about me but he's confused
because
   another girl maybe she does the same work as him
maybe
   a brunette or
   or she never wears make-up.

Tim Who is?

Rose Why did I do that? Argh!

Tim What?

Rose If I hadn't let him come he'd still want me and why
in my mouth? Such an amateur! Now he just thinks I'm
some slag he can
   FUCKIT!

Tim Rose

Rose Stupid
 useless
 dickhead dickhead / dickhead

She finds something to bang. Possibly her own head.

dickhead dickhead dickhead

Tim Rose Rose
 Hey
 come on
 Stop it.

Rose I've ruined it!

Tim No you haven't!

Rose YES I HAVE!

He comforts her.

Tim Shhhh.

They hold each other.

Rose What's *wrong* with me?

Tim Nothing! You're perfect!

Rose Why is he doing this?

Tim Because he's an idiot.

Rose No!

Tim Yes he is.

Rose I'm the idiot.

Tim You're gorgeous.

Rose I'm useless.

Tim So beautiful.

He moves his hand behind her neck.

Rose No I'm not.

Tim You are.

Rose Tim

Tim Sexy.

Kisses her hair.

Rose Tim!

Tim Ever since I first saw you

Rose What are you doing?

He is sort of groping her.

Tim I can't stop thinking about you.

Rose Stop it.

Tim All the time just

Rose Tim!

Tim thinking / about you all the time

Rose Tim. Tim! Stop it!

She breaks away.

What are you doing?

Tim Sorry. / I thought

Rose I thought you were my friend.

Tim I am.

Rose Are you?

Tim I love you.

Beat.

Is that
    I thought
    You said you loved me too.

Rose I have to go.

Tim Rose?

Rose Don't touch me! Don't
    I don't want to talk to you.

Tim Where are you going?

Rose I don't know.

Tim Are you OK?

Rose Snake.
    Deceiver.
    Serpent.
    What do you care?

    *She runs out. As she does so, one of her shoes comes
    off. She leaves it behind.*

Tim Rose wait!

    *Tim grabs the shoe – he nearly goes after her.
        The front door slams.
        Tim drops the shoe. Turns. Goes over to Nan. He
    picks her up.*

    He goes to smash her on the floor.

Fucking

    He squawks.

Why did you leave me?

    He hugs her to him.

How could you?

    Blackout.

THE KARAOKE BAR

A disco ball turns, pink light.
   Rose has been drinking. She sings a power ballad.
   *In one hand, she holds the microphone. In her other
hand, her remaining shoe dangles. Her feet are cut and
dirty.*
   Around her the voices start and move.

   twenty-twelve
   ninety-one
   one-hundred-per-cent genuine
   binge drinking
   twenty-four hour heating
   fully furnished
   gated
   no drug addicts
   eighty-eight
   no students
   young professionals
   no smokers
   this is a roomshare
   no smoking
   fully furnished
   no ball games
   two toilets
   lots of storage
   to do
   to get
   to be
   forget
   he hurt me
   pack your bags
   unattended on the
   underground two minutes

let me know how you
get off at Finchley Road
change platform
change jobs
change knickers
change money
change the world
phone a friend
I found your speech very
moving house
going down
coming round
overground
missing
a train
my mother
four years and still missing
children
wants children
wants
love from
I love you
I love her
I love him
I need him
I want her
I miss her
I love her
I need her
how tall
five minutes
how old
natural blonde
how green
twenty-twelve
forty-five women

a van in East London
West London
Central
District
Jubilee
Bakerloo
four minutes
two minutes
fifty-two passengers
no District and Circle
no service
no fat blokes
no ketchup
no gherkins
no Russians
no talking
no
no
I said no
no men
find flat
pick up stuff
sort out teeth
pay bill
call bank
have a wank
fall in love
get a bike
what do you do
get married
what do you do
have kids
where r u?
move to the country
what do you do
live happily ever after

two minutes
away
go away
out my way
move away from the platform edge
what do you do
hey darling
what do you do
hey sweetheart
who are you
hey someone
just someone
please someone
is anyone
anyone
hello?
hello?
is anyone there?

As she nears the climax of the song, Rose pushes the
heel of her stiletto into her left eye.
    Blood pours down her face.
    She does the same to the other eye.
    Blackout.
    Into:

17
CASSIE AND ROSE'S FLAT

VOICES

It's me
Hi
excuse me
no thank you
Hi

It's me
I want
beep

*Cassie opens a drawer in Rose's bedroom. Letters in
brown envelopes come flooding out, pouring, pouring,
until Cassie stands knee deep.*
    Blackout.

18
A HOSPITAL WAITING ROOM

Sounds of a hospital. A siren somewhere.
    Cassie is pacing up and down.
    Tim has just been to get coffee. He holds two.

Cas Thanks.

Tim No worries.

    *Cassie takes hers, puts it down and keeps pacing. Tim
    sits.*

Cas Fucking bastard.

    Beat.

What the fuck does he think? This has nothing to do with
him?

Tim I think the thing about / Mark is he just

Cas Please don't make excuses for him I actually can't
deal with it.

Tim It just
    it might not be his fault.

Cas I thought you said she gave him a blowjob?

Tim She said he
    in her mouth.

Cas And then what?

Tim I don't know. I think he had a shower. Thing is

Cas No!

Tim OK.

Beat.

It's
   nice to meet you I mean
   I guess that's a weird thing to say in the whatsit.
Circumstance. But I've heard lots about you.

Cas Off who?

Tim Off Rose.

Beat.

Cas I feel sick.

Tim Are you OK?

Cas I don't think I've ever been
   this
   look

She holds up her hands to him. They are shaking.

I just

She thumps her hand on her chest.

don't

She bangs the sides of her head.

I hate him. I want to fucking
   Why doesn't he care? Why do you always
   always find a way to make it not your fault? Eh?

He looks at her, helpless.

Get him to come. Call him. Tell him to come!

Tim He won't.

Cas I want to stab him.

Tim Cassie

Cas I want him to bleed. I want to stab him in his empty
gutless
arrogant body and just for once in his life
I want him to suffer!

Tim If it's any consolation
I think he does.

Cas No he doesn't.

Tim I mean
I know he doesn't know he does
or seem like he does
but I think
maybe
he does.

Cas I don't know what that means.

Tim No.

Cas I thought
you know
I actually believed

Beat.

Doesn't matter.

She sits.

Why did she do it?

Tim I don't know.

Cas What was she doing?

Tim (I just think)

I just think
for some people the world is good. You know?
But for other people . . .

He shrugs.
Pause.

Cas It's weird. How come they called you?

Tim I was her last dialled number.

Cas Oh. Right. Course.

Tim I went through her phone
when I got here
there was only four numbers in it: yours
mine
Mark's
and the *Daily Mirror* Astrological Helpline.

Beat.

Cas What about her mum or
she's got a dad hasn't she?

Tim The police tracked him down. Apparently he lives
on a pig farm.

Cas And?

Tim He can't leave the pigs.

Cas Oh.

Beat.

I got her off Gumtree.

Tim I know.

Cas That sounds awful, I just
I don't know what to do.

Tim Thing is

I mean
maybe when she wakes up, because
I've got some experience with
well
looking after people I thought

Cas Yeah?

Tim So she's not alone. I could. If she wants me to.

Cas I don't want her to be alone.

Tim Me neither.

Cas Yeah. I guess
you should just
see how it goes.

Tim OK. Yeah.

Cas It's very kind of you.

Tim No.

Cas No it is. You're a bigger man than me.

She looks at him.

I didn't

Tim It's OK.

Blackout.

19
A RECOVERY WARD: ROSE'S ROOM

Birds singing. Spring sunshine.
Rose is in a wheelchair. Looking out of a window.
There are still dressings on her eyes but she is much
better.
Three 'Get Well' cards adorn various places.

Mark is fussing with a vase of daffodils.

Mark Apparently you like daffodils.

Rose Really? Who said that?

Mark Tim did. Why is he taking so long?

Rose Sometimes there's a queue.

He looks at her.

Thanks for coming.

Mark Can't stay long I'm afraid. But Tim said you had news?

Rose Big news. But we want to tell together.

Mark Uh huh.

He checks his watch.

Listen
    Rose
sorry I haven't come sooner.

Rose It's OK.

Mark Felt a bit

Rose Doesn't matter.

Mark Just because

Rose Honestly Mark I haven't noticed.

Mark OK well that's good.

Mark checks for Tim.

Won't be ages will he? Only I have to be in London Bridge by twelve so

Rose He'll be quick as he can.

Mark OK.

Rose Tim says you got a promotion.

Mark Yeah that's right.

Rose And how's your girlfriend?

Mark My
Oh. Yeah. She's good.

Rose Does she work in marketing?

Mark Nah. No way. She's
a dancer.

Rose Really?

Mark Yeah.

Rose Where did you meet?

Mark Just out and about.

Rose A dancer.

Mark I know.

   Beat.

Rose I love him you know.

Mark What's that?

Rose Mark. I love him.

Mark You
Tim you mean.

Rose Course Tim. Who do you think?

Mark You said

Rose You're not jealous are you?

Mark Not really.

Rose Sorry things didn't work out between us.

Mark Um.

He pulls a face at her.

Rose But I'll always be grateful to you.

Mark OK.

Rose For bringing us together.

Cassie comes to the door. She stops.

Mark I'm just
glad it worked out for (you).

Cas Oh.

Mark Hey. Hi.

Rose Who is it?

Cas It's me.

Rose Cassie?

Cas Yeah. Hi.

Rose Hello!

Cas Sorry I didn't

Rose Oh Cassie! This is Mark! He came! Mark this is
Cassie!

Mark Hi. Yeah we've met.

Rose Oh yes of course you have!

Cas Ages ago.

Mark At the flat.

Cas How are you?

Mark I'm great thanks. You know. Ticking along. You?

Rose Cassie come in. Let's hang out.

Cas I / think maybe

Rose Don't you think they sound the same?

Cas Who?

Rose Mark and Tim.

Mark No.

Rose I noticed a couple of weeks ago. Because you went to college together. I think my hearing's got better. More acute. Like a seventh sense.

Cas How have you been?

Rose Uh. Brilliant thanks! Come in! Tell me about you. What's happening?

Cas I'm fine. I think I should come back later. Tim didn't say you'd have visitors.

Rose It's not visitors! It's Mark! And we need you here. We've got something to tell you.

Cas Don't you two want to hang out?

Rose Don't be silly. Sit down. Let's chat.

Cas OK.

Rose Did Tim call you? What did he say?

Cas He was very mysterious.

Rose Come and sit.

Cas I can't stay long.

Mark Rose says you've been brilliant, Cassie.

Cas Does she?

Rose You have. She has! And Cassie's got news of her own, Mark. Did Tim tell you?

Mark No.

Cas No! / We're not

Rose Cassie's having a baby!
  Can you believe it?

Mark I
  Really?

  Beat.

You're having a baby?

Cas Yeah.

  Beat.

Mark Congratulations.

Cas Thanks.

Rose She's building a human. Isn't it amazing? She met
this guy in a bar, pissed. Can you believe that? A completely
random one-night stand and yet they conceived a human
being. Don't you think that's like
  a miracle? And Cassie says that's why she can't get rid
of it because it's so unlikely to have happened she just
thinks this baby is somehow important.

Cas I / didn't say

Rose Like Gandhi.

Cas I didn't / mean like

Rose Can you believe that?

Mark When was this?

Cas A while ago. / Ages ago.

Rose Before my accident. She'd just got pregnant then
but we didn't know did we?

Cas No.

Rose Can you believe out of something so
　　Meaningless
　　you can get
　　Actual
　　Life?!

Mark Can we

　　He points outside.
　　　While Rose is speaking Mark and Cassie conduct
　　their silent conversation.

Rose You know the most amazing thing about babies is
you can drop them from a great height and because
they're not scared and their bones are all soft
　　they don't break. Don't you think that's extraordinary?

Cas (Why?)

　　He mouths.

Mark (I want to talk to you.)

　　She mouths.

Cas (What about?)

Mark Please?

Cas Yeah. That's amazing.

Rose Are you OK Mark?

Mark Yeah I'm cool, I'm just

Rose Cassie's going to try and bring it up in London
aren't you Cassie? I think that's very brave. Taking a
buggy on the bus.

Mark That hat.

　　He points to Cassie's belly.

Is it mine?

Cas No.

Rose What hat?

Mark Are you sure?

Rose What hat?

Cas Very.

Mark So there was
another
person?

Rose What other person?

Cas There was.

He nods.

Rose What person?

Mark I believe you.

Rose What hat?

*Somewhere out in the corridor, a door slams shut.
They jump.*

Rose What was that?

Cas Just something outside. It's OK.

Rose It scared me.

Cas It's OK.

*A brief pause.
Mark looks at Cassie.*

Mark You given up smoking then I take it?

Cassie looks at Mark.

Cas Yeah.

Rose All you needed was the right motivation. Wasn't it?

Cas Seems like it.
   Yeah.

   Tim enters.

Tim Am I OK to come back in? Hi.

Cas Hi.

Rose Timmy!

Mark Here he is!

Rose Quick come in! Mark has to go in a minute.

Tim Hi Cassie.

Cas How's it going?

Tim Good, yeah. Here you go, Rosie. Can of Coke.

Rose Thanks Timmy. Ooh.

Mark So come on then.

   Tim kisses Rose.

Let's have this news. You got two minutes. We're on
tenterhooks (!)

   He grins at Cassie.

Rose Timmy Muffin and me
   are moving to Eastbourne.

   Beat.

Tim We're moving in together.

Cas Oh! That's
   brilliant.

   Mark laughs.

Tim By the sea.

Rose Get a place by the sea.

Tim Hear the gulls.

Rose Eat cockles.

Tim Walk on the beach.

Rose Listen to the sound of the waves.

Mark You're joking aren't you?

Cas I think it sounds lovely.

Mark What about your new job?

Tim I've handed in my notice.

Mark Took you ages to get that job.

Rose Timmy's not destined for the rat race, are you
Timmy?

Tim I was only doing it to save money.

Mark You said you liked it.

Tim I didn't hate it.

Mark You're leaving the flat?

Tim I know

Mark I thought

Tim Sorry.

Mark No I mean
  do what you want. Be glad to have the place to myself
again if I'm honest I just –
  are you sure it's what you want?

Tim I'm sure.

Mark When are you going?

Tim I'm going to head down there at the weekend. Start
getting sorted.

Mark This weekend?

Tim She'll be out in a few days.

Mark Yeah but the weekend? You need longer. You can't just
    by the weekend. What about
    I dunno

Tim We don't have anything planned do we?

Mark Not planned. I just
    I dunno.

Tim I can come back and visit.

Mark Do what you want I just
    I want to make sure you're doing the right thing. You know? Just seems a bit impulsive.

Tim It's what I really want.

Mark I just

Cas I think it sounds like a good move. Be good for you.

Mark All I'm saying is I think you should give London another chance, mate. You know? You haven't even been here a year. You need to get used to it. Once you're used to it
    I promise
    you'll never want to leave.

Tim I don't want to get used to it.

Mark It's the best city in the world.

Cas He wants to live by the sea.

Rose We both do.

Mark No I know I just

Tim Rose needs me.

Mark Yeah but . . .

He is about to say something. But:

I don't know. No. Yeah. It's great. It's great. I'm happy
for you. Nah it's
    brilliant listen I'd best shoot off if that's OK?

Tim Already?

Mark Yeah mate I've got a fucking presentation at
twelve and I'm running late as it is so if you don't mind,
ladies?

Rose Thanks for coming.

Mark Nice to see you again Cassie. And
    good luck with that baby!

Cas Thanks.

Mark Nice to see you Rose glad you're on the mend and
    good luck with everything

Rose You too!

Tim I'll come out with you.

Tim comes over to Mark.
    Mark pulls Tim into his arms. Hugs him.
    For a second it seems like Mark might cry. Then:

Mark Cool. Right. Get off me you faggot. Come on.
Let's go! Bye then. / See you girls.

Rose Thanks for the flowers!

Mark Bye! No worries. / Bye.

Rose See you!

Mark and Tim leave.

I've got to stop saying that.

Cassie sits back down. She reaches for Rose's hand.
Rose smiles.

Isn't this a happy ending though? I mean
    me and Tim. In love. Moving in together. You having a
baby. It's all so
    perfect.

Cas Is it?

Rose If it's a girl you can call it Rose. If you want.

    Cassie laughs.

You should think about it though. Maybe do some
calculations. Is it going to have your surname?

Cas I guess so.

Rose Rose Grey. Dunno. Sounds like a really bland shade
of paint. Talking of which. Can you believe I was so in
love with that man? You know he had an eggshell-
coloured flat? How did I let that go by? Boring bastard.

Cas Yeah.

Rose You couldn't stand him. You knew right away. You
always said he was a wanker. Remember?

Cas Ha. I remember. Yeah.

Rose And he had a really bad sense of humour. I
remember he told me this really weird story once about
how on his first day at boarding school all the new boys
had to go into this courtyard thing and take their clothes
off and all the older boys leaned out the windows and
pissed on them from above?! I was like, is that a joke?
Because it's not very funny.

    Cassie goes to the window. Looks out.

Are you OK? You seem a bit
    Beat.

Cas Oh God I hope it's not a boy.

Rose The baby?

Cas Dunno.

Rose You could call it
Raoul. I always wanted a boy called Raoul.

Cas Might call it Dick.

Rose Really?

Cas After its father.

Rose laughs.

Rose Dick Grey. Yeah. That's OK. I think he'll grow up to be a politician.

Cas Fuck that. I hope it's a girl.

Rose Me too.

Cas I don't think I could love a boy.

Rose Yeah you could.

Cas That's it though. I really don't know if I could.

Rose Anything is possible, Cassie. Remember? I told you didn't I?

Cas Told me what?

Rose Anything is possible.

Cas Right. Sorry.

Rose You just have to believe.

Blackout.

20

EASTBOURNE PIER

Tim stands on the end of Eastbourne Pier.
  Seagulls caw etc.
  It is warm.
  Tim holds Nan.
  He unscrews the lid and takes it off.

Tim I remember one day I banged my head in the garden
I must have been about five
  and Paul from next door was laughing at me for crying
and I came in the kitchen and you were there and you
said it's OK Timmy. Don't cry. And you got the butter
you were making cakes with and starting putting it on
my head and I remember even then I was thinking
  butter?
Is that what you do for a bump on the head? But then
there was your fingers all soft on my head where it hurt
and
  and it didn't matter so much because
  you made it better. And then one day
  and I feel like
  I'm just so
  sorry if you ever felt scared or
alone or if I didn't say the right things I just kept
thinking you'd get well again. Like some miracle would
  I don't know. Because I did ask. I did hope. I did pray.
All the time. But it didn't work. Did it? And
  anyway Rose says I've got to let go. So
  I want to say thank you. For everything. And
  What I mean is
  thank you for how you loved me. And I'm not
  forgetting you. I'll never forget you. Ever. I couldn't.
You know? I just

I wish I could be in your room one more time with the telly on *Coronation Street* and you in your chair smoking a fag and I could say this
properly
like I should have at the time but
Rose says if I say it now. You'll hear. Somehow. She says you'll hear. Can you hear?
Nan?
Are you there?

Beat.

If you're out there?
Give me a sign!
Any sign!
Just tell me you're there!

He shuts his eyes.
  Waits.
  Nothing happens.
  He reaches into the urn.
  Brings out a handful of ash.
  Contained within the ash are loads of cigarette ends.
Tim stares in wonder, holds his hand up to the sky.
  Music plays.
  Dandelion clock heads float past on the breeze.
  Tim beams.

Blackout.